#TATA STORIES

ADVANCE PRAISE FOR THE BOOK

'In my younger years, I was privileged to begin my career with the Tatas. I have interacted with only four people mentioned in the book—J.R.D. Tata, Ratan Tata, Sumant Moolgaokar and Darbari Seth. However, I have heard many stories during my time in the Bombay House, the office and on the shop floor speaking to Shri R.M. Lala. True to its word, this book will take you down memory lane into the world of the legendary Tatas, who will always hold a special place in my heart.'—Sudha Murty

'No theory on leadership can teach you better than real stories of leadership. #*TataStories* by Harish Bhat is the proof.'—Piyush Pandey

'Tata's value system is the stuff of legend, and it was quite fascinating to read about the people who institutionalized these values. These forty carefully crafted stories are richly anecdotal, revealing, insightful and a joy to read. We learn how Tata's incredible line of business leaders and institution-builders served the nation, while also gaining insights into some of their best practices which are as relevant for today's fast-moving digital world as they were for an earlier era. Harish Bhat captivates our minds, and gives us a rare glimpse into the heart of the Tata way.'—Sunil Kant Munjal

'Harish Bhat's #*TataStories*, written in his inimitable breezy style, holds valuable lessons on what creates a "business with a purpose". In the book, we will not only hear the back stories of the Taj Hotel, Tata Steel, Indian Institute of Science, Tata Cancer Hospital, TIFR and NCPA, but also learn about the supercomputer Eka, the toilet-roll-audit of J.R.D., Jubilee Diamond's steel connection, Nani Palkhivala's anonymous eye donation and the sixteen-egg omelette of Russi Mody. The book can be an ideal textbook for a course on what is today called "conscious capitalism". Read it to get inspired.'—Ambi Parameswaran

'This is a book to be savoured one story at a time. Through many little vignettes and anecdotes, Harish Bhat takes us on a journey that showcases business at its very best. This is not a book about strategy or business triumphs but about the humanness that has been such as essential part of the Tata ethos. It is a particularly timely book for it reminds us of the nobility that enterprise is capable of, from its smallest actions to its role in the task of nation-building.'— Santosh Desai

'The Tata Group is unique not just in India but the world. Its story has been told and retold several times. But what Harish Bhat has done is to show its human side by gathering together a wonderful series of anecdotes involving the people who founded and ran the group . . . These are not only interesting in themselves but are also inspiring in their reiteration of a value system.'—Anil Dharker

#TATA STORIES

40 TIMELESS TALES
TO INSPIRE YOU

HARISH BHAT

BUSINESS

An imprint of Penguin Random House

PENGUIN BUSINESS

USA | Canada | UK | Ireland | Australia
New Zealand | India | South Africa | China | Singapore

Penguin Business is part of the Penguin Random House group of companies
whose addresses can be found at global.penguinrandomhouse.com

Published by Penguin Random House India Pvt. Ltd.
4th Floor, Capital Tower 1, MG Road,
Gurugram 122 002, Haryana, India

First published in Penguin Business by Penguin Random House India 2021

Copyright © Harish Bhat 2021

All rights reserved

26 25 24

The views and opinions expressed in this book are the author's own and the facts
are as reported by him which have been verified to the extent possible, and the
publishers are not in any way liable for the same.

ISBN 9780670095322

Typeset in Adobe Garamond Pro by Manipal Technologies Limited, Manipal
Printed at Thomson Press India Ltd, New Delhi

www.penguin.co.in

*Dedicated to my colleagues at the Tata Central Archives,
who preserve the inspiring history of the Tata Group
with such love and care*

Contents

Introduction

The First Story

This is a storybook with a difference. It contains many inspiring stories which are wide-ranging in their scope, all of them drawn from the history of the Tata Group, a remarkable institution which has a legacy stretching back more than 150 years.

Tata is the largest Indian corporate house, and one of the most visible India-headquartered conglomerates in the world. Over 700 million consumers across the world use Tata products and services because of their consistent quality, enduring appeal and the trust that Tata is privileged to have earned over the past fifteen decades.

Dancing across this long arc of time are thousands of beautiful, astonishing Tata stories, many of which can inspire and provoke us, even move us to meaningful action in our own lives. These stories bring to vivid life the extraordinary longevity, vibrancy and success of Tata. But at their essence, they are simple, moving stories of great teams, men and women, which hold deep lessons for all of us.

But there is always a first story, and this is the story of why the Tata Group exists.

The Story of Jamsetji Tata

This story begins in a small one-storey house in Navsari, a town in Gujarat, in the western part of India. Here, on 3 March 1839, a son was born to Nusserwanji Tata, who came from a Parsi Zoroastrian priestly family. This boy was Jamsetji Tata, founder of the Tata Group. When he was thirteen years of age, Jamsetji moved to live with his father in Mumbai.

He studied at Elphinstone College there, and developed a deep love of reading. His favourite authors were Charles Dickens and William Makepeace Thackeray, and he also enjoyed the humorous writings of Mark Twain. His books provided him a wonderful window to the world.

That window expanded even farther when he joined his father's firm. Then, in 1868, he established a private trading firm with a capital of Rs 21,000. That was the start of the Tata Group. A few years later, in 1874, he founded his first major industrial venture, the Central India Spinning, Weaving and Manufacturing Company Limited, at Nagpur. This venture is popularly referred to as Empress Mills.

Empress Mills was an extraordinary endeavour, and it also revealed this young man's future promise. He was convinced of the benefits of long-stapled cotton as the best raw material for these mills, and therefore devoted a lot of his attention to improving the cultivation of cotton in India. He also quickly and confidently invested in new manufacturing innovations, such as the ring spindle, which substantially improved the output of the factory. Thus, Empress Mills soon became a very profitable enterprise.

But mere profits were not the real reason why Empress Mills was so special. Here, in the nineteenth century, when human resource development was an unheard-of concept, Jamsetji Tata introduced a gratuitous pension fund for the workers of the mills, in 1887. This was the first of its kind in the country. In 1895, he established an accident compensation scheme for workers. In 1901, he introduced a Provident Fund scheme for his workers. This was the first time ever in India that this concept had been introduced. Each of these schemes, devised specifically for employee welfare, were pioneering innovations in Indian industry, which established a new way of doing business.

Speaking in 1895, he explained this new way: 'We do not claim to be more unselfish, more generous, or more philanthropic than other people. But, we think, we started on sound and straightforward business principles, considering the interests of our shareholders our own, and the health and welfare of our employees the sure foundation of our prosperity.'

Nation-building and Pioneering

Jamsetji Tata soon applied this same philosophy to every business he established. Businesses should strive hard to be profitable, but they exist to serve a larger need—that of the community. As he expanded the canvas of his activities, the meaning of community expanded to envelop the entire nation. The love of India soon became the driving force of his life.

This deep and abiding love led him to conceptualize India's first integrated steel mill, the country's first grand luxury hotel, and an Indian university of science education and research. He set out his vision of creating an organization where the 'community is not just another stakeholder in business, but is, in fact, the very purpose of its existence'. A vision that has remained the guiding North Star for the Tata Group.

The Tata Trusts are the best illustration of how this philosophy has been put into action. For the past 125 years, they have contributed consistently to the community, investing significantly in education, health, livelihoods, art and culture.

These public charitable trusts own 66 per cent of the equity shares of Tata Sons, the parent company of the Tata Group. As a result of this unique ownership structure, a significant proportion of the profits of Tata Sons flow to the Tata Trusts, which in turn invest these funds back into the community. In the words of J.R.D. Tata, who was chairman of the Tata Group for over fifty years, this ensures that 'what came from the people has gone back to the people, many times over'.

If giving back to the community has been the guiding North Star, pioneering new enterprises has been the restless ship on which Tata has sailed towards this horizon. Since inception, the Tatas have pioneered multiple businesses which are important to the nation: India's first integrated steel plant. India's first major hydroelectric power company. India's first commercial airline. The company that put India on the global IT services map. The first indigenous Indian car. Branded iodized salt, which changed the way India consumes its food. Branded jewellery, which has transformed one of the country's largest markets. And many more.

These pioneering businesses, each of them relevant to their day and age, have pursued excellence in their respective industries. They have served important consumer needs even as they have upheld principled corporate behaviour, and contributed to the communities which they are part of. They have constantly fuelled the Tata ship for over 150 years, and continue to do so.

Tata Stories

From these strong and unique pillars of pioneering and nation-building come the fascinating stories that are narrated in this book.

You will find in these pages many stories from the life of the founder, Jamsetji Tata, himself. You will also read stories that come from later decades, when the group was steered by his successors, including Sir Dorabji Tata, J.R.D. Tata and Ratan Tata.

You will also discover stories that involve many other legendary Tata leaders, including Lady Meherbai Tata, Charles Perin, Nevill Vintcent, Bobby Kooka, Dr John Matthai, Sumant Moolgaokar, Russi Mody, Darbari Seth, Nani Palkhivala and Xerxes Desai.

There are stirring stories of nation-building, which involve iconic national leaders such as Swami Vivekananda, Mahatma Gandhi and Jawaharlal Nehru. There are also exciting stories of innovation, and breakthrough Tata products that were born of these pioneering pursuits.

At the heart of many of these tales, you will find endearing human stories, of people driven by passion and purpose, of men and women who treasured their dreams and reached beyond their grasp to convert their visions into reality. Stories of grit, persistence, restlessness, resilience, failure and success.

These stories are narrated in no particular chronological order. As you read them, you will move back and forth in history, but in a seamless sort of way, because the stories are bound together with the same distinctive Tata glue. There is a unique pleasure in moving up and down so many years in such a story-time machine.

By no means are these stories comprehensive, either. I have chosen to narrate a set of forty Tata stories that have appealed most to my imagination, based on my current knowledge. Undoubtedly, there are many more equally inspiring stories still waiting to be told.

Story Time

This brings me to the subject of why we read stories. We read stories because they are interesting, and they captivate our minds. That is why stories have been narrated and heard with such joy, ever since the beginning of mankind. You could choose to sit back and enjoy the Tata stories in this book with just this objective. There are so many interesting characters, facts, twists and turns that populate them—all of which are truly wonderful in their own right.

We also read stories because they inspire us and move us. You may find that some of these Tata stories particularly resonate with you—they may be deeply inspiring, from your own perspective. Perhaps the lessons that these specific tales put forward are of particular value in your own life. This too, is a very good reason to read these stories and reflect on them.

Taken collectively, these stories delve deep into the heart of the Tata way, and illustrate why the Tata Group continues to be so successful, more than 150 years after it was founded by Jamsetji Tata. If you are a student of business history, or a young entrepreneur wishing to establish a sustainable enterprise, this is also a good reason to reflect on these tales.

But perhaps the best reason to lose yourself amongst all these stories is the magic that they can create in your mind and heart. The magic of emotions that stir your heart, of a penny that suddenly drops in your mind. We seek some magic in our lives, don't we, and that's what beautiful stories are all about.

Without further ado, happy Tata story time.

1

Dear Swami Vivekananda: Part I

On 14 July 1893, at 3.40 p.m., the ocean liner *SS Empress of India* set sail from the Japanese port of Yokohama. It was on its voyage to Vancouver, in British Columbia, Canada. This was a graceful ship, painted white, with two buff-coloured funnels banded with black paint at the top, and sporting three tall masts. The ship could accommodate 770 passengers—120 in first class, fifty in second class and 600 in steerage. On this ship were two passengers who would, in their respective ways, shape the future of India.

Walk back into history with me, cross the deck of the ship, and meet Swami Vivekananda—at that time a relatively unknown young monk. He was travelling to America and wished to speak at the World Parliament of Religions in Chicago, scheduled for September that year. Over the past five years, he had led the life of a *parivrajaka,* a wandering monk. In 1892, upon meditation on a rock at Kanyakumari, he had 'a vision of one India', of organizing monks for the progress and upliftment of the nation. He was now travelling to America to deliver his message at one of the greatest global gatherings of all religions, representing India and Hinduism.

Also on board the ship was Jamsetji Tata, a well-known merchant of Mumbai and founder of the Tata Group. He had been to Japan for discussions on shipping, and during this visit, he had also seen with admiration the commendable progress made by Japan in several areas, including industry and sericulture. Now, he too, like the Swamiji, was on his way to Chicago, to visit the World Columbian Exposition where advancements in various areas, including science and technology, were being showcased. This great fair was being held in 1893 to celebrate the 400th anniversary of Christopher Columbus's arrival in the New World.

Indeed, like Christopher Columbus, Swami Vivekananda and Jamsetji Tata were both avid explorers themselves. Both were curious men, and both were constantly thinking, fervently restless, about the future of their nation. It was destiny, perhaps, that they got talking to each other on board the ship. This was a sea voyage of nearly twelve days and there was plenty of time for conversation and reflection.

Unfortunately, we do not have any first-hand details of the conversations between these two legendary men. How interesting and revealing it would have been to listen to them and catch a glimpse of their thoughts about India and its future.

Jamsetji Tata was greatly impressed with Vivekananda, and is known to have later told Sister Nivedita, one of Swamiji's best-known disciples, that when 'Swami was in Japan everyone was struck by his likeness to Buddha'. From some secondary sources, Swamiji is reported to have inquired of Jamsetji why he imported Japanese matches into India. He then pleaded with the industrialist to instead set up a match factory in India to create employment and preserve national wealth.

It is quite possible (though we have no evidence of this) that Jamsetji spoke about his own plans for India's industrialization, including early Tata ventures such as Empress Mills in Nagpur, which had already made a deep impact by then. I think that Jamsetji may also have outlined quite passionately the details of the scheme he had established just a year ago, in 1892, to send a few chosen Indian students to England for higher education. He had created an endowment fund specifically for this purpose, and he was very proud of his scholars.

A research paper, which has examined details of this voyage, says it is likely that Swamiji spoke to Jamsetji Tata about his various plans, including the ones for 'organizing monks for industrial purposes' to ensure the advancement of the country. This thought must have inspired Jamsetji Tata—he had already been thinking about higher education in industrial and technical areas to impart self-reliance to future generations of Indians.

Indeed, this conversation with Swamiji must have stayed on in Jamsetji Tata's mind because five years later, in 1898, when he was ready with his ambitious plans for the establishment of the Indian Institute of Science, he wrote to Swami Vivekananda. Here is the letter he wrote.

23rd November, 1898
Esplanade House, Bombay

Dear Swami Vivekananda,

I trust you remember me as a fellow-traveller on your voyage from Japan to Chicago. I very much recall at this moment your views on the growth of the ascetic spirit in India, and the duty, not of destroying, but of diverting it into useful channels.

I recall these ideas in connection with my scheme of a Research Institute of Science for India, of which you have doubtless heard or read. It seems to me that no better use can be made of the ascetic spirit than the establishment of monasteries or residential halls for men dominated by this spirit, where they should live with ordinary decency, and devote their lives to the cultivation of sciences—natural and humanistic. I am of [the] opinion that if such a crusade in favour of an asceticism of this kind were undertaken by a competent leader, it would greatly help asceticism, science, and the good name of our common country; and I know not who would make a more fitting general of such a campaign than Vivekananda.

Do you think you would care to apply yourself to the mission of galvanising into life our ancient traditions in this respect? Perhaps, you had better begin with a fiery pamphlet rousing our people in this matter. I should cheerfully defray all the expenses of publication.

With kind regards,
I am dear Swami
Yours faithfully
Jamsetji N. Tata

In the meantime, the ship *SS Empress of India* reached its destination in Vancouver on 25 July 1893 after a splendid voyage. If we could look back in time, we would have seen both these great men disembark from it at this bustling seaport in British Columbia. They would soon head towards Chicago, carrying great dreams and aspirations for the nation they loved with all their heart.

2

Dear Swami Vivekananda: Part II

Jamsetji Tata's letter to Swami Vivekananda reflected his passion for his ambitious scheme of establishing an institute of science for India. He had great belief in his countrymen and believed that with the right higher education, Indians would achieve great heights of success in the areas of science and technology, which were so critical to the country's progress.

But this would require a university that focused on science education, which could provide large numbers of Indian students an opportunity to complete their higher studies within the country. In September 1898, two months before he wrote his letter to Swamiji, Jamsetji Tata made public his plans for this institute. He also committed an endowment of Rs 30 lakh towards this project. In 1898, this was a fabulous sum of money; a gift of this nature had previously been unheard of.

This generosity brought forth great praise from his countrymen. A prominent Indian of that time, writing in *The Hindu* newspaper, said—'Mother Bharati has long been crying for a man among her children, and in Mr Tata she has found the son of her heart.' Yet it was clear that, despite Mr Tata's generous offer, the establishment of a world-class science institute would require far greater financial support than was available. Mr Tata needed to urgently raise funds. And the British, who were ruling India at the time, were not so forthcoming. Lord Curzon, the then viceroy of India, acknowledged Mr Tata's generosity and public spirit but also put forward many questions and expressed some misgivings. The question the nation faced was—would this great project now be stalled? Would Indians get the opportunity they deserved for higher education in science?

Meanwhile, Swami Vivekananda had returned to India after a triumphant voyage to the United States of America. In 1893, after his voyage by ship, briefly described earlier, he had reached Chicago and famously addressed the Parliament of Religions there. 'Sisters and brothers of America,' he had begun his stirring speech after more than two minutes of standing applause. With great zeal, he had put forward to Americans the essence of Hinduism, and his country's ancient heritage and rich culture. He had completed very successful lecture tours in the USA, UK and Europe, and left a great impression everywhere. In 1897, he had returned to India and founded the Ramakrishna Mission in Kolkata.

Swami Vivekananda had sparked great interest and pride across the Western world in India's spiritual heritage. At the same time, he knew that promoting science and industrialization was essential for economic progress and the upliftment of the nation. He was terribly upset by the economic misery of his countrymen and had spoken of the need 'to organize monks for industrial purposes, that they might give the people the benefit of this industrial education, and thus elevate them and improve their condition'.

Therefore, Jamsetji Tata's letter and scheme of establishing an institute of science must have resonated greatly with Swami Vivekananda. Jamsetji had requested Swamiji for a pamphlet supporting and evangelizing scientific education and had offered to defray all publication expenses of the same. We do not know whether a pamphlet was actually printed, but in April 1899, *Prabuddha Bharata*, the monthly journal of the Ramakrishna Order, which had been started by Swami Vivekananda, published a wonderfully detailed page of observations, which were virtually a reply to Jamsetji Tata's appeal. It would appear that these observations were written either by Swamiji himself or by someone who had been advised by him.

Here are some extracts from the observations published in *Prabuddha Bharata*. They reflect Swami Vivekananda's resounding support for Jamsetji Tata's appeal, and there is an exhortation to the entire nation to back this project.

We are not aware if any project at once so opportune and so far-reaching in its beneficial effects was ever mooted in India, as that of the postgraduate research University of Mr Tata. The scheme grasps the vital point of weakness in our national well-being with a clearness of vision and tightness of grip, the masterliness of which is only equaled by the munificence of the gift which it is ushered to the public.

Mr Tata's scheme paves the path for placing into the hands of Indians this knowledge of nature . . .

By some the scheme is regarded as chimerical, because of the immense amount of money required for it, to wit about Rs 74 lakh. The best reply to this fear is: If one man— and he not the richest in the land—could find 30 lakh, could not the whole country find the rest? It is ridiculous to think otherwise, when the interest sought to be served is of the paramount importance.

We repeat: No idea more potent for good to the whole nation has seen the light of day in modern India. Let the whole nation, therefore, forgetful of class or sect interests, join in making it a success.

Here is a unique example of a great Indian spiritual master lending his unstinted support to an ambitious project being put forward by an Indian industrialist. What a beautiful example of two fellow travellers who once embarked on a voyage on the same ship now walking the same path for the progress of their beloved nation.

Eventually, adequate funding was obtained and the Indian Institute of Science was born in Bangalore in 1911. It is today the nation's pre-eminent science university and one that has built a formidable reputation worldwide. In Bangalore, many locals still fondly refer to it as the Tata Institute.

Sadly, neither Swami Vivekananda nor Jamsetji Tata lived to see the birth of this institute. Swamiji attained samadhi in 1902. Jamsetji Tata passed away in 1904. But there is no doubt that their blessings and presence permeate every corridor, lecture hall and laboratory of this famous institution. They lived, toiled and died for the love of their nation, for the India of their dreams. May their thoughts and deeds inspire us in our own lives.

3

OK TATA, OK SUMO

Travel by any road in India, and it is very likely that you will soon see a TATA truck carrying essential items such as grains, pulses or construction material. Chances are also high that you will find, painted on the back of the truck, the two words 'OK TATA'. This lovely phrase is painted by truck drivers and local painters who are proud of their colourful truck art, and not by the company.

I have often wondered, why OK TATA? The best answer I have found is in the life of Sumant Moolgaokar, the brilliant engineer–technocrat who headed Tata Motors (then called TELCO) for several years. J.R.D. Tata appointed him director-in-charge of TELCO in 1949. In 1954, the company entered into a partnership with Daimler-Benz of Germany for manufacturing trucks. The partnership with Benz was for a period of fifteen years, thereafter TELCO went forward on its own, and 'we never looked back after that', in the words of Moolgaokar.

He was a stickler for perfection, and wanted every Tata truck to be of excellent quality. He would not tolerate the '*chalta hai*' attitude that we sometimes associate with shoddy Indian work. During the period of collaboration with Daimler-Benz, once a week, all the parts rejected by the German technicians were displayed publicly, and a post-mortem was held on what had gone wrong with each of these components. This was often a painful exercise for the Indian engineers, but it ensured that quality moved up quickly to German levels.

Arun Maira, who was a director of TELCO during the 1980s, narrates yet another example of Sumant Moolgaokar's drive for perfection. TELCO Pune had designed and fabricated the country's first fully automated transfer machine for manufacturing cylinder heads for engines. It was a feat of engineering excellence. Maira and his engineers believed that they had done a superlative job, and they proudly invited Moolgaokar to see this machine for himself. Moolgaokar inspected the machine with great interest. The engineers were perhaps now expecting to be complimented on their achievement.

However, Moolgaokar said nothing. Instead, he returned to the office, and called for Maira. There, he told him, 'Maira, did you notice the hydraulic pipes? All are not vertical. Please see for yourself.' Maira returned to the new machine, and indeed he now noticed that some of the pipes were not vertical; they were slightly out of line. When he reported this, Moolgaokar turned around and told him, 'Maira, trifles make for perfection. And perfection is no trifle. You will strip the machine and build it again, with everything perfect this time.'

Moolgaokar famously said, 'Do not accept second-rate work. Expect the best, ask for it, pursue it relentlessly, and you will get it.' He also asked for the best ancillary parts from all his suppliers, and thus played a big role in elevating engineering standards across the country. Tata trucks continue to be known for their robust quality.

But 'OK TATA' has much more to it than excellent quality alone. There was a period in the 1970s when Tata trucks were in short supply. Hence, the trucks were being sold by middlemen at a premium of around Rs 40,000 per truck. Moolgaokar naturally faced a lot of pressure from various quarters to raise prices and take advantage of the constrained supplies. Tata Motors, under his leadership, stood steadfast, and refused to profiteer by doing so. Later, Moolgaokar was asked by the historian R.M. Lala why he took this decision. Here is his answer: 'Profits should come from productivity and not by raising prices in a favourable market,' said Moolgaokar, 'our greatest asset is customer affection.'

I discovered yet another reason for 'OK TATA' during my visits to the Tata Motors plant in Pune. Adjacent to this factory, I found a beautiful lake full of migratory birds. Very unusual for a factory that makes trucks and cars, I thought to myself. I was intrigued, and read up some history. When land was first bought for this factory, Moolgaokar insisted that trees be planted around the factory, as well as an artificial lake to store and supply water for the nurturing of these trees.

At that time, he was criticized for spending Rs 15 lakhs to create the lake. But today, this man-made wetland of 245 acres holds 60 million gallons of water, has dense green cover with over 1,50,000 trees, has supplied thousands of fruit trees to surrounding villages, and is a beautiful haven for over 150 species of migratory birds and sixty types of butterflies. For him, the larger environment was as important as the product itself.

J.R.D. Tata once said about this fascinating initiative: 'We did not have to create a lake and plant trees to produce a truck. But we did. What I am most proud about is not the making of steel or trucks, but our social concern.'

J.R.D.'s observations about Moolgaokar reflect his esteem for the man: 'He built the factory, he built the men, he built the technology . . . he began to build a new edifice for the future . . . a magnificent factory and a magnificent force that elicited pride.'

When Moolgaokar passed away in July 1989, his colleagues and newspaper editorials referred to him not merely as a brilliant technocrat or an inspiring leader of people, but as a nation builder par excellence. Building India for the future was the mission that drove him. He often said that he would like Tatas to belong to the nation: in other words, to always do what is right for the country.

Think of all this, and think of Sumant Moolgaokar when you next see 'OK TATA' on a truck. No wonder Tata Motors named one of its first crossover vehicles as 'Sumo', in tribute to him—borrowing the first two letters of his first name and second name, respectively. OK TATA, OK SUMO.

4

The Astronaut and the Pioneer

Kalpana Chawla is a national hero in India and one of the most celebrated women of our times. The first woman of Indian origin to go into space, she first flew on Space Shuttle Columbia in 1997 as a technical specialist and robot arm operator. An asteroid, as well as a satellite, have been named after her. NASA has dedicated a supercomputer to her memory, and she has been an inspiration to millions of young Indian boys and girls who wish to achieve big and meaningful things in their own lives.

Kalpana Chawla lost her life at the young age of forty years in the Space Shuttle Columbia disaster in 2003. The spacecraft she was travelling in disintegrated during its re-entry into the Earth's atmosphere and all seven crew members unfortunately perished. India, and the world, mourned and cried.

Sometime after her demise, Kalpana Chawla's family wrote to the chairman of the Tata Group, Ratan Tata. This was a unique letter because it contained some special memorabilia. There was a crew-autographed group picture of the Space Shuttle Mission STS-87 (her first Space Shuttle Mission), a pair of medallions commemorating her two space journeys, and an old black-and-white photograph. This was the photograph of J.R.D. Tata's inaugural mail flight, which Kalpana Chawla had carried along with her on her first mission into space.

Here was a heartfelt tribute from a young girl to her hero. To a man who had inspired her to travel all the way from a small north-Indian town called Karnal, to the far reaches of outer space—J.R.D. Tata. This young girl had carried into space, on her very first mission, an old sepia photograph of a pioneer whose deeds had sparked her own ambitions. Yes, she was telling us that we need similar people and their deeds to inspire us. Such inspiring legends light a fire in our hearts that gives us the courage to aim for the stars.

Kalpana Chawla had always admired J.R.D. Just before her second trip into space, she had told reporters that he had been her inspiration. She said, 'What J.R.D. Tata had done during those years was very intriguing and definitely captivated my imagination.'

Let us dial back for a moment to 1982, the year in which Kalpana Chawla left India for the USA to pursue her master's in aerospace engineering. In that very year, J.R.D. Tata did something special that inspired millions of Indians. He piloted the flight commemorating the fiftieth anniversary of India's very first commercial flight, which he had himself flown in 1932 from Karachi to Mumbai. In 1932, that inaugural mail flight had launched India's civil aviation industry but at that time J.R.D. was a strapping young man. Now, in 1982, J.R.D. Tata was seventy-eight years of age, and yet he was determined to go ahead and pilot the commemorative flight himself.

Faced with a reluctant board of directors that was unwilling to let him fly at this advanced age, he wrote to them firmly enough: 'I have recently got myself fully checked up medically, including hearing and eyesight, and have been declared fit in every way . . .' Three weeks before the date of the flight, J.R.D.

had suffered a minor heart attack but recovered quickly. Seeing his steely determination, his consulting physician and cardiologist decided to permit him to fly because the emotional strain of abandoning his cherished dream could have been even greater than the physical strain of flying.

On 15 October 1982, J.R.D. Tata, seventy-eight years old, took to the skies and flew once again from Karachi to Mumbai to recreate that pioneering first flight of fifty years ago. His old friend Captain Vishwanath was his co-pilot. All the way from Pakistan to India flew J.R.D., the grand patriarch, a man who had done his best for his nation throughout his lifetime. As he neared Mumbai, two Air Force helicopters escorted the little plane for a short distance—their salute to the grand old man—and then they departed. J.R.D. Tata landed at the Juhu aerodrome in Mumbai at 4 p.m. sharp, having circled in the air for a few minutes to avoid landing early. There he was, as punctual as ever.

He spoke briefly to the gathering after landing the aircraft. 'This flight of mine today,' he said, 'was intended to inspire a little hope and enthusiasm in the younger people of our country, that despite all the difficulties, all the frustrations, there is a joy in having done something as well as you could, and better than others thought you could.'

One youngster amongst them, among the many he inspired with such hope and enthusiasm, was Kalpana Chawla. She flew into space and made us all proud, sparking off the dreams of millions of young Indians.

The treasured photographs that Kalpana Chawla's family sent to Ratan Tata are now displayed in the Tata Central Archives in Pune just outside the beautifully recreated office of J.R.D. Tata. This was done in line with her family's request so that this tribute to the man who inspired her rests just outside his door.

Both Kalpana Chawla and J.R.D. Tata, the astronaut and the pioneer, are no longer with us. But their legendary achievements and deeds will provide us with strength forever. What will Kalpana and J.R.D. inspire each of us to do today? How will we strive to achieve our own dreams, for our own fulfilment, and the greater good of our nation and humanity?

5

Tata Indica, India's Own Car

Cars have always been symbols of patriotism and pride, and they have also been an engine of rapid economic growth in nations across the world. Brands like Toyota, Rolls-Royce, Mercedes-Benz, Ford, Fiat and Hyundai have been flagbearers for their respective countries.

By the early 1990s, India had launched spacecraft and missiles but it did not have a car that it could call its own—a car that had been designed, developed and produced within the country. Would India ever have that car worthy of its national stature and pride?

Ratan Tata, who was then chairman of the Tata Group and Tata Motors, stood up in 1995 to express his ambitions for the nation. He said, 'We'll have a car with the Zen's size, the Ambassador's internal dimensions, the price of a Maruti 800 and with the running cost of diesel.' Many sceptics and naysayers refused to believe in an Indian car. But Mr Tata was determined; he and his team forged ahead with the Tata Indica. Indeed, the name of this car, Indica, spelt pride in the nation.

In many ways, this courageous decision brought to mind the determination of Jamsetji Tata, more than a century ago, to create India's first integrated steel plant. At that time, he had to override the cynical reaction of the British, who thought that Indians could never make their own steel. Now, history was repeating itself.

If the Indica was to be world class, its design had to be comparable with the best. Skilled and passionate engineers from the Engineering Research Centre of Tata Motors, Pune, undertook this exciting challenge in association with the Turin-based design house, I.D.E.A. The car had to be futuristic and sleek in its design but it also had to rise to Ratan Tata's challenge of providing enough space for an Indian family. The transmission system was developed entirely in-house, adding new capabilities to a company that had no background in cars.

When the design for the Tata Indica was eventually unveiled, the reactions it elicited were euphoric. Everyone agreed that it was clearly ahead of its time. It was very distinctive compared to the other cars of that period and had unmistakable international appeal. 'This was breakthrough styling, and we knew it as soon as we saw it!' was the spontaneous reaction of many shop-floor engineers at Tata Motors.

Then there was the question of the car manufacturing facility itself. A new manufacturing unit could have cost more than $2 billion at that stage, a huge amount that possibly would have rendered the project a non-starter. Here, again, Ratan Tata and his team at Tata Motors took a road less travelled and it ended up making all the difference. They searched around the world and found a disused Nissan plant in Australia, which was offered to them for sale at barely one-fifth of the cost of a new plant. Engineers of Tata Motors carefully dismantled this plant—brick by brick—carried it across the seas, and rebuilt it in Pune. It took just six months to accomplish this Herculean task.

The Tata Indica was manufactured not just with technological precision but also with great pride and love. Ratan Tata used to visit the Indica manufacturing facilities quite often. On one such early visit, he noticed operators fixing the rear strut of the car manually. The operator would have to bend down 600 times to complete this operation on 300 cars each day. Ratan Tata called his managers immediately. 'How can we expect our men to do this throughout their lives? Surely it will damage their health. We must provide an automation solution on priority.' The engineering department rose to the occasion and quickly developed a fixture to semi-automate the operation. Operators remember this fondly even today.

The Tata Indica was launched in 1998 to fabulous bookings and response. But it soon encountered several engineering and quality problems—uneven tyre wear, belt noise and defective pulleys—which came in for a lot of criticism. Consumer complaints escalated, and rival companies began to write premature epitaphs for the Indica. There is, of course, no dearth of condescending minds, both Western and Indian, that never miss an opportunity to take potshots at India and other developing nations.

In the midst of this intense backlash, Ratan Tata led from the front and steered the company's efforts towards the improvements that were required immediately. Deep within the team there was great resilience, undying hope and a strong commitment to making this pioneering venture, India's very first car, a great success. The team worked very hard, and it succeeded. A new, robust Indica was ready by 2001 with all the key quality problems addressed and completely eliminated. It was launched as Tata Indica V2, with the punchline 'Even more car per car'.

The impact of the Indica V2 was extraordinary and immediate. It marked not just the revival of the Indica but also its brilliant success. It became the fastest-selling automobile in Indian history when it completed the sale of 1,00,000 cars in less than eighteen months. Despite an overall economic slowdown in 2001, it recorded a handsome growth of over 46 per cent in that year. The reputed television programme *BBC Wheels* declared the Indica the 'best car in the Rs 3 lakh to Rs 5 lakh category'.

The confidence was back. There had been a hiccup but the team at Tata Motors had proven itself more than capable. India's first indigenously designed car had conclusively been a great success.

Why did Ratan Tata take on the challenge of making India's own car? Listen to his words: 'I had a strong conviction,' he says, 'that our engineers, who could put a rocket into space, could produce our own car. And when we took up the challenge, we went out and got expertise wherever it was necessary. Everything we had in it was ours. So, to me [the Indica] was a great feeling of national achievement.'

This feeling of national pride and achievement, of contributing to nation-building—may it inspire each of us in what we wish to do with our own lives. Fulfilment comes from our contributions, however small or large, to our community and our nation. That is my foremost lesson from the story of Tata Indica, India's own car.

6

Gandhiji in Jamshedpur

The steel city of Jamshedpur was teeming with excitement in August 1925. Mahatma Gandhi was coming to visit the town where India's first integrated steel plant had been established by Jamsetji Tata. This would be a unique event—the man who was leading the charge for Indian independence visiting an industrial city which had taken a step towards economic independence.

Mahatma Gandhi knew of Jamsetji Tata's enterprise. Indeed, in 1905, soon after Jamsetji's passing, he had written in the *Indian Opinion* newspaper, 'In whatever he did, Mr Tata never looked to self-interest. He never cared for any titles from the Government, nor did he ever take distinctions of caste or race into consideration . . . His simplicity was remarkable. May India produce many Tatas!'

The Mahatma had been keen to visit the steel city himself, and now he was responding to a special invitation from Dinabandhu C.F. Andrews, who was at that time a labour leader in Jamshedpur. He had sought Gandhiji's guidance to resolve some labour issues. Interestingly, many years later, Subhash

Chandra Bose would also head the Tata Steel Workers' Union in Jamshedpur, but that is the subject of another story.

Gandhiji arrived in Jamshedpur and was shown around the steel factory. I can imagine how eagerly workers in the factory would have milled around to see the great man walk briskly by their furnaces that had begun proudly producing steel for the nation. He also visited the township and wrote later in his journal: 'This town owes a debt of gratitude to the courage of Jamsetji Tata.' But he went on to say: 'However, what can one see of such a large factory in two days?'

At the Director's Bungalow, he completed talks with R.D. Tata (father of J.R.D. Tata), and three outstanding labour matters were resolved after some discussion. It is remarkable that Gandhi took the time and effort to travel all the way to Jamshedpur to help bring these matters to a successful conclusion.

Then, in the evening, he addressed a mass meeting on the maidan behind the TISCO Institute, now called the United Club. This was a huge gathering, attended by over 20,000 people. A sea of humanity stood waiting for the Mahatma to arrive, and he did not disappoint them. In fact, Gandhiji delivered a fine and spirited speech, which was both moving and inspiring. Here are some excerpts.

> It was my ambition to see one of the greatest—if not the greatest—Indian enterprises in India, and study the conditions of work there. But none of my activities is one-sided, and as my religion begins and ends with truth and non-violence, my identification with labour does not conflict with my friendship with capital. And believe me, throughout my public service of thirty-five years, though I have been obliged to range myself seemingly against capital, capitalists have in the end regarded me as their true friend.

I am told that though so many Europeans and Indians live here (together), their relations are of a happy character . . . It is the privilege of both of you to be associated in this great enterprise, and it is possible for you to give Indians an object lesson in amity and goodwill . . . you will carry your amity outside your workshops and both of you will realize that you have come to live and work here as brothers and sisters, never regarding another as inferior, or oneself as inferior. And if you succeed in doing that, you will have a miniature Swaraj.

Gandhiji also narrated to the audience an anecdote about how his connection with the Tatas began.

In South Africa, when I was struggling with the Indians there, in the attempt to retain our self-respect and to vindicate our status, it was the late Sir Ratan Tata who first came forward with assistance. He wrote me a great letter, and sent a princely donation—a cheque for Rs 25,000 and a promise in the letter to send more, if necessary.

This was a reference to the spontaneous donation that Sir Ratan Tata, younger son of Jamsetji Tata, had made in the year 1909. In his letter of 29 November 1909, referring to Gandhi's struggle in South Africa, and offering the donation, Tata had said: 'It is a struggle of which the people of this country have every reason to be proud.'

Sir Ratan Tata then made a few more contributions to the South African struggle, a total of five instalments between 1909 and 1912, taking the total amount he donated to Rs 1.25 lakh—a very large amount in those days. This led Gandhiji to write in an editorial: 'Mr. Ratan Tata has outdone himself . . . The total given by Mr Tata therefore amounts to L5,000 (in the local currency)—a fortune in itself. Mr Tata's munificence shows not only his large heartedness, but also his keen appreciation of the struggle . . . the moral effect of such help on those who, from prejudice, are opposed to us, is also obvious.'

This background, as well as the recent visit to the magnificent steel plant and the township of Jamshedpur, must have been at the forefront of Gandhiji's mind as he ended his speech with the following stirring words, which must have moved every member of the Tata Steel family present in the audience that day:

> May God grant that, in serving the Tatas, you will also serve India, and will always realize that you are here for a much higher mission than merely working for an Industrial enterprise.

These are timeless and inspiring words spoken by the Mahatma. Indeed, they touch the essence of what Tata stands for, the very philosophy with which Jamsetji Tata founded the enterprise in 1868—which, coincidentally, was just a year before Gandhiji was born.

Mahatma Gandhi visited Jamshedpur two more times—in 1934 and 1941. The Tata Group, and Jamshedpur, are blessed that the Father of our Nation visited the town thrice during his lifetime.

Many years later, J.R.D. Tata spoke for millions of Indians when he described Gandhi as 'by far the greatest personality and, to this day, the most extraordinary human being I have ever met; he inspired in me, as in most people, a mixture of awe, admiration and affection, combined with some scepticism about his economic philosophy, despite which one would follow or support him to the end, come what may.'

Our nation won its freedom because our forefathers followed and supported Mahatma Gandhi's mission right until the end. His visits to Jamshedpur are a fondly treasured page in the vast log of that great voyage.

7

A Titan of Our Times

Xerxes Desai, founder of the Titan Company, is one of the most fascinating business leaders of our times. A graduate of New College, Oxford, where he had studied philosophy, politics and economics, he joined the Tata Administrative Service, the central management cadre of the Tata Group, in 1961. He spoke beautifully crafted English, with an equally charming British accent, and possessed a wide range of eclectic interests, including aesthetics and design, Western classical music and French wine.

Before he founded Titan in 1985, he had already worked with the Tata Group for over two decades, initially with the Taj Group of Hotels. Here, he had led the construction of the new tower of the Taj Mahal Hotel in Mumbai. He had also spearheaded the development of the Taj Fort Aguada Resort in Goa, well before Goa had been discovered by the world at large. Thereafter, he had been deputed to CIDCO (City and Industrial Development Corporation of Maharashtra), where he had served as a project manager for the Vashi township. Post this stint, he had also served as managing director of Tata Press.

But it was in Titan that Xerxes Desai came into his own. He scripted the extraordinary launch of Titan watches, which took India by storm in 1987. This was a transformational event in Indian marketing history. With a dazzling range of new timekeeping designs which Indians had never experienced before, and the new technology that accompanied them, Titan soon established clear market leadership and won over the hearts and wrists of millions of Indians.

At the heart of this success were Xerxes Desai's vision and courage. He decided to launch only quartz watches in a market that knew only mechanical watches, because he firmly believed that quartz was a superior technology for accurate timekeeping. Also, quartz watches contained fewer components which allowed them to be slimmer than the mechanical watches, and hence, they were far more suited to sleeker and more fashionable designs. Brushing naysayers aside, he did not launch a single mechanical watch. It was all quartz. Elegant, stylish and breathtaking.

He launched these watches with brilliant advertising, including the creation of a famous signature tune for Titan using Mozart's 25th symphony—which he found uniquely uplifting and therefore a perfect fit for the beauty of the watches. In a country like India where very few people had any interest at all in Western classical music, this Titan tune soon became as popular as Bollywood music. Once again, Xerxes Desai and his advertising partner, Ogilvy, Benson & Mather, had been courageous in choosing a path that few people would dare to take, and they struck gold.

But at the heart of Xerxes Desai's vision was the creation and elevation of an entire community. Perhaps he had in mind Jamsetji Tata's clarion call for Jamshedpur, nearly a century ago, when he set about creating new factories to manufacture watches at Hosur in Tamil Nadu. Titan was a joint venture between the Tata Group and the Government of Tamil Nadu, and it had committed to generating employment in the state. But it faced a big challenge in finding hundreds of workers with the required skill sets for the complex segment of watch manufacturing.

What the company did then was fascinating. It went to schools in the smaller towns and villages of Tamil Nadu looking for young boys and girls who had passed the class ten exam and were over sixteen years of age. It met the principals of these schools and convinced them that a job in Titan would be good for their students. No one had heard of Titan but the fact that it was a Tata company perhaps helped. Since this was the first time many of these young people would be leaving their homes, Titan set up temporary houses where foster fathers and mothers would look after them for some time. From small towns such as Namakkal and Krishnagiri came hundreds of bright-eyed, eager youngsters, many from needy families, walking into a new Titan factory to manufacture and assemble wristwatches for the first time in their lives.

Titan provided these youngsters with the intensive training that was required. Over the next few years, it amazingly transformed them into skilled watchmakers. The company also created for them a factory campus and a township, which are beautiful and energizing. Designed by the legendary architect Charles Correa and painstakingly landscaped by Xerxes Desai himself, these campuses at Hosur continue to be happy homes to thousands of Titanians. So many of them have now studied further, completing their graduate and postgraduate studies. They have pursued beautiful dreams for their families and built strong careers with the Titan company, which is their home.

Xerxes Desai retired from Titan in 2002. He continued his close association with the Titan School, which he had lovingly established for employees' children, at Hosur. In fact, one of his last engagements, before his unfortunate demise in June 2016, was an interaction at his beloved school. Titan, the company that he founded, has gone on to become one of the country's best-known lifestyle companies, and also one of the most successful companies of the Tata Group—with great brands such as Tanishq, Fastrack, Sonata, Titan Eye Plus and Taneira. Etched deep in its memory and high in its admiration is the image of Xerxes Desai.

I attended Xerxes Desai's funeral, which was also held in Hosur. Thousands of people moved in a long, slow line behind the hearse as it wound its way from the watch factory to the dusty funeral ground. On that hot afternoon, it appeared that more than half the town had turned out to say a fond, tearful goodbye to a man they admired and loved. After all, this was the community that he had helped create. Thousands of livelihoods, happy families and beautiful dreams—is there a better gift that a man could give the world?

8

The Creche at Empress Mills

Empress Mills at Nagpur, one of the very first enterprises of the Tata Group, was opened on 1 January 1877, more than 140 years ago. This mill produced textiles of high quality, due to which it prospered greatly, and became the most important factory of its kind throughout India. But the greatest contribution of Empress Mills to our nation is the visionary standards it set for worker welfare.

In those distant days, when childcare for working women was virtually unheard of in India, Empress Mills established two crèches for the babies of the women employed there. Girls who worked half-time in the mill could attend classes in reading, writing and needlework. A primary school was established to provide education to the small boys who brought meals to their mothers, who were working in the mill. It is easy to imagine a small boy running in with a lunch box for his mother, and being promptly escorted by the Mehtaji to a classroom to study the alphabets. It is, however, difficult to imagine that all this happened over a century ago.

That was not all. For older children, the mills established two factory schools, towards the upkeep of which the directors made a financial contribution. For women, a maternity benefit allowance was put in place in 1921. Women who had been employed for eleven months or more were provided two months' paid maternity benefit. Seven night schools were established, where languages were taught, as well as music and dance. A weekly lecture was instituted for the benefit of the workers, which was a unique collaboration between the mills and the local YMCA (Young Men's Christian Association).

Four gymnasia were also set up for exercise and good health, and sports was made an integral part of life at the mills. A cinematograph was installed in the compound of one of the mills, using which thousands of people could be entertained. Employees enjoyed free medical facilities, with separate dispensaries for men and women. Each year, a Health Week was organized to highlight various diseases and how workers could keep themselves and their families safe.

In 1921, the Jamsetji Tata Girls' High School was established in Nagpur, with a generous grant from Empress Mills and its directors, to take forward women's education, which was a particular area of focus. An endowment was created to ensure that the school obtained a regular annual income. This magnificent school, which came up opposite the Jumma Talao, continues to flourish until this day.

Many of us take the concept of a provident fund for granted today. PF, as it is popularly called, is now enforced by law in India, and is an integral part of our monthly payslips. But did you know that Empress Mills was the first institution in India to introduce the concept of a provident fund, many decades before it was legally mandated? Way back in 1901, the mills established a provident fund scheme for its employees. In 1887, a gratuitous pension fund had been established, and, in 1895, an accident compensation scheme as well. To further help the workers, a cooperative credit society was also set up around the same time.

Jamsetji Tata, founder of the Tata Group, was proud of Empress Mills. For him, it was a labour of love. It was not merely a high-quality cotton-spinning mill, but a caring institution which provided the best facilities for the welfare of its people. In 1895, speaking at the opening of a new extension of Empress Mills, which was by then a flourishing enterprise, he talked about the prosperity that the mill had begun enjoying, because of its top quality and excellent reputation with all stakeholders. Then, he went on to speak about what lay at the core of the enterprise, saying: 'We do not claim to be more unselfish, more generous or more philanthropic than other people. But, we think, we started on sound and straightforward business principles, considering the interests of our shareholders our own, and the health and welfare of our employees the sure foundation of our prosperity.'

In the same address, he spoke about some of the specific steps that Empress Mills had taken for employee care. For instance, on the subject of ventilation in the mills, he said: 'We have paid the greatest attention to sanitary arrangements, and constantly studied the question with a view to improve them. We have provided fans for ventilation, humidifiers to prevent the effects of extremely dry air, khus-khus *tatties* for cooling the rooms, which must, by the nature of our business, get hotter in the hot weather. But still we are not quite satisfied with what we have done. We are about to try a new scheme in the shed. This scheme, we hope, will be a great improvement upon what we have hitherto done, and we are confident that if it succeeds in nothing else, it is sure to succeed in one thing—and that is in giving an equally distributed supply of free, fresh and pure air to our workpeople.'

It is fascinating to see from this address how immersed Jamsetji Tata was in every aspect of worker welfare. To him, this was of the highest importance. He went on to say: 'For all these arrangements, we do not claim any credit. They have all been adopted with a view to do good to ourselves, knowing full well that our good lies in the good of those with whom we come in contact in business, or on whom the success of our work entirely depends.' In other words, welfare of workers is essential to the success of the enterprise.

Built on these strong foundations, Empress Mills continued to enjoy great prosperity. By June 1920, the total profits of the mills were fifty times the original capital, and shareholders had gained splendidly, including bonus shares. Jamsetji Tata, who founded these mills, has been called the father of Indian industry. He went on to achieve many great things for India, including the establishment of Tata Steel at Jamshedpur, the Taj Mahal Hotel in Mumbai, the Tata hydroelectric project in the Western Ghats and the Indian Institute of Science in Bangalore. But it can be safely said that he began his life's work at Empress Mills, Nagpur.

Jamsetji Nusserwanji Tata (1839–1904), founder of the
Tata Group, the man who never stopped dreaming for his nation

'The Four Partners' (clockwise from left): Jamsetji N. Tata, founder of the Tata
Group; R.D. Tata, father of J.R.D. Tata; Ratan Tata, the younger son of the
founder; and Dorabji Tata, the elder son

Jamsetji Tata's letter to Swami Vivekananda dated 23 November 1898, seeking his support for the establishment of the Indian Institute of Science, Bangalore (digitally enhanced)

A view of the Taj Mahal Palace Hotel, Mumbai, before the construction of the Gateway of India. The Taj Mahal Palace Hotel was inaugurated in 1903. Construction of the Gateway of India was completed in 1924.

A view of the great dam at Walwhan near Lonavla. This marvellous dam stood at a height of 86.5 feet, with a length of 4449 feet. Construction began in 1911, over 100 years ago.

Courtesy of Tata Central Archives

Courtesy of Tata Central Archives

Lady Meherbai Tata, a feminist icon, shown here wearing the magnificent Jubilee Diamond, which is twice as large as the legendary Kohinoor. This diamond was once used to save Tata Steel from collapsing.

J.R.D. Tata at the Juhu Aerodrome, Bombay, on 15 October 1932. The first historic commercial air mail flight of the Indian subcontinent had just landed, piloted by J.R.D. Tata himself. Seen in the photograph are (from left to right) Nusserwanji Gazdar, Capt. Homi Bharucha, J.R.D. Tata, Nevill Vintcent and two officials of the postal service. This is also the iconic photograph that Kalpana Chawla carried into space.

J.R.D. Tata and Pandit Jawaharlal Nehru were, as the historian R.M. Lala puts it, 'once close friends, later distanced by ideology'. From left to right: Sir Ardeshir Dalal, J.R.D. Tata and Pandit Jawaharlal Nehru

Mahatma Gandhi and Babu Rajendra Prasad on a visit to
Jamshedpur in 1934. The Father of the Nation visited the
steel town thrice during his lifetime.

Ratan N. Tata drives the first Tata Indica off the assembly line at the Tata Motors
plant in Pune in 1998.

EDGE

THE SLIMMEST WATCH IN THE UNIVERSE

reddot design award
winner 2013
for Best Product Design.

1577TL01A from the Edge collection • Titanium casing
• Sapphire crystal glass on dial and back cover • Ultra-thin 1.15mm movement • Black Toscana leather strap

TOLL-FREE HELPLINE : 1800-266-0123 I www.facebook.com/TitanWatchesIndia

Available in leading Titan oulets across 32 countries.

Courtesy of Titan Company

The Titan Edge, a technological marvel that was proudly designed and manufactured in India. This photograph is an advertisement for one of the watches of the Titan Edge family, the Edge Skeletal, which also won the prestigious Red Dot Design Award for Best Product Design in 2013.

Xerxes Desai hands over a memento to J.R.D. Tata at the inauguration of the Titan watch manufacturing facility in Hosur, Tamil Nadu, on 11 March 1988.

One of the most memorable days of my life. In 1995, Darbari Seth, a legend of the Tata Group, came home to see our baby daughter, Gayatri. My parents, wife and I—all in the picture above—were moved, and delighted.

9

The Tata Silk Farm

Indian silk is beautiful, desirable and luxurious. An important and interesting episode in India's rich silk story resides in one small corner of Bangalore, in a place called the Tata Silk Farm.

Jamsetji Tata, founder of the Tata Group, was convinced that the silk industry could be of great benefit to India because Indian conditions were suitable to cultivation of the silkworm. He believed that India could become famous for silk. During a visit to Japan in 1893, he was impressed by how well the Japanese had developed scientific sericulture, including intense care of the soil. He came back to India, determined to establish India's finest silk manufacturing unit.

Jamsetji chose Bangalore for his silk farm because the temperate climate in this city resembled that of Japan. He put forward his scheme for the creation of a flourishing silk industry to the dewan of Mysore, Sir Seshadri Iyer. Mysore Silk was well known since the time of Tipu Sultan, and had often also been exported from India to European countries. However, the industry had declined in recent years. Eventually, with the dewan's support, Mr Tata bought the necessary land in the southern part of Bangalore and established the Tata Silk Farm.

As with all his ventures, Jamsetji wanted the very best for India. So he appointed Japanese managers for the farm who were well-skilled in sericulture—a couple named Mr and Mrs Odzu. He imported reeling machinery from Japan to ensure the finest manufacture, and was happy to note that this equipment was simple, efficient and easy to use. Most importantly, he wanted local Indians to quickly become skilled in the business of making silk so that they could themselves build a flourishing local industry.

To ensure this, the Tata Silk Farm offered free instruction to apprentices for a training programme that lasted at least three months. It covered a range of areas including the rearing of silkworms, cross-breeding, disease prevention, preservation of cocoons, creation of silk and packaging. A supervisor who knew English and Hindi was also appointed, to ensure appropriate interpretation of what the Japanese experts said. Very soon, from the agile fingers of Indians emerged silk of the highest quality. Silk woven in this farm was sent to Europe where experts declared it to be of very fine quality, and the best from India.

The farm soon became a big success, and Jamsetji tried to purchase additional land to expand the project, but he was unable to obtain further help from the Government of Mysore in this regard. However, the Tata Silk Farm provided a big impetus for the revival of the local silk industry. The Government of India, encouraged by the excellent quality reports emanating from Europe, established two more silk farms after consulting Mr Tata.

In the course of these discussions, Mr Tata revealed to them his true motive in establishing the Tata Silk Farm, which was to impart skills and generate employment for Indians.

Here is an extract from a letter he wrote to the inspector general of agriculture way back in 1903: 'The principal keynote that has impressed me much is that you have as your principal aim to train picked natives of our country in all departments of science and agriculture. Such should be the end and object of all sympathetic persons who are at the head of all Government Departments. I have always in my limited sphere endeavoured to keep this aim of training our native talent, and am always prepared to offer all the help and facility to those who so deserve it.'

In fact, some of the giants of Indian sericulture, such as Appadorai Mudaliar and Laxman Rao, were among the Tata Silk Farm's first trainees. Many years later, in 1949, the Central Silk Board was also established in Bangalore, taking on the role of evangelizing the development and growth of the silk industry in India.

After Jamsetji Tata passed away, his sons requested the Government of India to take over the Tata Silk Farm, since they were preoccupied with other larger businesses of the group, such as steel and electric power, which required significant focus. However, the government did not agree because they had already established other farms based on the same model which were functioning quite well by then. Eventually, the farm was given to the Salvation Army, who had established schools of sericulture for needy segments of society, and therefore had knowledge of this industry.

The Salvation Army successfully enlarged the Tata Silk Farm, and it soon became a model for the entire country. As a tribute to the founder of the farm, the new owners retained the 'Tata' name, and developed the project with great enthusiasm. This led to the further spread of the silk industry across India, with many more ventures being established not just in Bangalore, but in north India as well.

Acknowledging this positive impact, the Commissioner of the Salvation Army, Frederick Booth-Tucker, wrote in 1912 to Burjorji Padshah, a close associate of Jamsetji Tata, and later a Tata director: 'The impetus thus given to the silk industry in India can hardly be over-estimated . . . In not distant days, when silk will have become to India what it is already in such countries as Japan, China, France and Italy, the name of the man who launched the enterprise will be held in grateful remembrance by those [who] will have been benefited by his forethought and labours.'

Many years later, the unit was converted to a vegetable farm to feed an orphanage. Later, the rapid urbanization of Bangalore city put further pressure on the activities of the farm. Today, the farm no longer exists, but this area, which is located in the Basavanagudi neighbourhood of Bangalore, is still fondly referred to as the Tata Silk Farm.

More than a hundred years later, the wheel of silk has come a full circle. Taneira, a Tata product, curates and offers exquisite silk sarees today. It is working with silk weavers across India and hopes to play a useful role in rejuvenating this important industry for the future.

10

The Great Dam at Walwhan

Today, come with me to Walwhan, a small, picturesque town nestled in the Western Ghats of India, not far from Mumbai city. Walk with me through lush green trees all the way to the magnificent dam that sits on the Indrayani River. Stand here for a moment and look around; see the shimmering lake and dam in front of you. This is one of the most beautiful spots on earth. It is also home to a piece of India's history.

Here, in 1915, the Tata Group inaugurated the country's most ambitious hydroelectric project to supply clean electric power to the city of Mumbai. A few years earlier, Jamsetji Tata, founder of the Tata Group, had spoken about the heavy monsoon rains in the area and remarked, 'All this water from the Western Ghats is wasted. We should harness it to produce hydroelectric power.' Such a project also attracted him because it would help make the industry of the city less dependent on coal, which was not good for the environment, and was also expensive. By 1915, Jamsetji Tata was unfortunately no more, but his dream was just about to become a reality.

The great dam at Walwhan, built by Tata Power (then called the Tata Hydroelectric Supply Company), was a commendable engineering feat. This marvellous dam stood at a height of 86.5 feet, with a length of 4449 feet, and a dam volume of 64,00,000 cubic feet. It was only a little smaller than the original legendary dam on the Nile River, constructed at Aswan by Sir William Willcocks. Many people had thought that such a scheme was inconceivable in India, but the Tatas had determined to forge ahead.

Despite some initial hesitation in the firm, Sir Dorabji Tata, Jamsetji's son and the second chairman of the Tata Group, shouldered this responsibility with great energy and enthusiasm after the demise of his father. He travelled across the country, successfully persuading rulers of Indian states to subscribe to shares of the company which would implement the project. When Lord Sydenham laid the foundation stone of the dam in 1911, he rightly said of this giant venture: 'It symbolizes the confidence of Indians in themselves, their willingness to be associated with a project that is somewhat unfamiliar in this country.' Indeed, these were some of the first confident steps in India's development.

Around the same time, two more adjacent dams were built by Tata Power at Lonavala and Shirawta. Giant pipes were laid, which were around 7 feet in diameter, to carry water from all these dams to the foot of the Western Ghats. Water rushed through these pipes, along a steep fall of 1734 feet, to the power station at Khopoli. Here, hydraulic energy was converted into electrical energy using massive generators. The electricity thus generated was initially transmitted to a receiving station in Mumbai, and, thereon, through transmission lines, electric current was supplied to the mills of Mumbai.

This was a complicated project, which involved many engineering difficulties, including the construction of an artificial river, the laying of pipes which were hewn into the solid rocks of the hills, and anchoring of these pipes to deal with issues arising from the tropical heat. Nothing of this magnitude had ever been attempted in the past in India. It was, by any standards, pioneering work.

Eventually, on successful completion of the project, Lord Willingdon, governor of Bombay, switched on the power at the receiving station in Parel, a locality of Mumbai, on 11 February 1915. Addressing Sir Dorabji Tata, he said, 'It must be a source of pride and satisfaction to you, Mr Chairman, and to your brother, to find that today you have established in India another magnificent and permanent memorial to your father's great services to his country.'

Speaking at the same event, Sir Dorabji Tata reflected on the overarching spirit and goal that gave birth to this ambitious project. 'To my father,' he said, 'the hydroelectric project was not merely a dividend-earning scheme; it was a means to an end . . . the development of the manufacturing power of Bombay. It is in that spirit that we have carried out the fruitful ideas he bequeathed to us.'

In one stroke, these dams and hydroelectric projects provided power to drive more than one-third of all the mills in Mumbai. It was hoped that with this supply of clean, hydroelectric power, Mumbai would soon become a 'smokeless city', free from the grimy coal that textile mills were burning at that time for their energy requirements. In addition, these mills also gained significantly from inexpensive electricity, leading to increased demand, which in turn led to further expansion of the hydroelectric projects of the Tata Group.

It is pertinent to note here that Jamsetji Tata and his son, Dorabji Tata, did not ever hesitate to obtain the best global expertise in industrial matters such as the construction of dams because they knew that the India of that time needed people with the requisite technical knowledge. At the inauguration, Dorabji paid tribute to three Western engineers, R.B. Joyner, Alfred Dickenson and H.P. Gibbs, whose dedicated efforts made this entire project, including the Walwhan Dam, possible. H.P. Gibbs went on to become general manager of the company.

There is an interesting and important footnote to the story of the Walwhan Dam. Not only has this scheme supplied clean electric power to the city of Mumbai for over a century now, it has also actively engaged in the conservation of the mahseer, a fish which was on the verge of extinction and continues to be an endangered species. For over four decades now, Tata Power has successfully bred this fish in captivity in the Walwhan Lake. The hatchery breeds around 2.5 to 3 lakh baby fish each year and releases them back into the lake. This is perhaps one of the biggest wildlife conservation projects in India after Project Tiger. Conservation is such a worthy sister to clean energy, the purpose for which the Walwhan Dam was originally established.

Today, Tata Power, the company born at Walwhan over a century ago, continues to proudly supply uninterrupted power to the city of Mumbai. Meanwhile, come along with me, let's visit Walwhan, and watch history pass by.

11

Tetley and Tata:
A Defining Moment

In February 2000, more than twenty years ago, BBC ran a lead article that made India proud. 'Tetley bagged by India's Tata', said the headline. It went on to say: 'Tetley Tea, inventor of the tea bag and maker of the traditional English cuppa, is being bought by Tata Tea of India. The deal to buy the world's second largest producer of teabags is worth 271 million UK pounds, and is the biggest acquisition in Indian corporate history.' The Tata Group had just created history once again. But behind this historic moment lay a fascinating story.

This tale begins with a veteran of the Tata Group, R.K. Krishna Kumar, popularly known as KK. In the 1990s, he was managing director of Tata Tea, and he had been reflecting on the fall of the Berlin Wall. To KK, this signalled a new world structure and a new vision for the company he led.

Over the previous decade, KK had already achieved some significant breakthroughs in Tata Tea. He had steered its transformation from a small tea plantation company to a branded tea major. This strategic effort was led by Darbari Seth, chairman of the company, and by KK. In the mid-1980s, the company launched two major 'plantation packed' brands of tea—Tata Tea and Kanan Devan—which took the market by storm. Within a decade, Tata Tea had captured a handsome 15 per cent of the Indian branded tea market, giving a tough time to the market leader, Unilever.

After this rapid success in India, what was next for Tata Tea? KK had scanned the long list of international tea companies, and dreamt of an Indian firm making a splash in the global markets. He knew that organically building a strong consumer brand from scratch in new countries would be very challenging. There was the distant possibility of acquiring an international tea brand, which could obviate this risk at one stroke, but could this ever be done? No Indian company had ever acquired a global brand for this kind of money until then.

Recalling those days, KK said, 'Vision often makes its first appearance disguised as a pipe dream. This has happened several times over in the history of the Tata Group. It is the true calling of leadership to seize such dreams, and transform them into splendid reality.'

An opportunity to seize this dream arose when Lyons Tetley, part of the large Allied Lyons Group, began buying instant tea from Tata Tea in 1990. Allied Lyons had a presence in foods, tea, coffee and breweries. They owned Tetley, the world's second-largest brand of tea. The management of Lyons Tetley soon acquired a lot of respect for Tata Tea's expertise in tea and this led to the establishment of a joint venture in Kochi for the manufacture of teabags. Both companies happily discovered that they were totally committed to the world of tea. They had begun dating but there was no marriage on the horizon yet.

Four years later, in 1994, the first serious proposal was on the cards. Allied Lyons, owners of the Tetley brand, announced their merger with Pedro Domecq to create a liquor multinational, Allied Domecq. They were now keen to focus on liquor, and exit the non-core tea and coffee business. When KK heard this news, his eyes immediately lit up. Here was a rare opportunity to acquire Tetley, one of the world's leading tea brands. But back then, Tetley was so much bigger than Tata Tea. The resources required for such an acquisition would be staggering. How could he even dream of such a proposition?

But KK was supported in his enthusiasm by Ratan Tata, who had become chairman of the Tata Group in 1991, and by senior directors, including Darbari Seth and Noshir Soonawala. They saw the compelling logic of going global and felt the opportunity deserved to be explored.

A Tata Tea team reached London in early 1995 to pursue the acquisition. I was privileged to be a junior member of this team. We studied mountains of documents over countless prawn sandwiches and cups of tea. There were also long discussions with the Allied Domecq management and with bankers who could potentially fund the acquisition. Consensus was achieved on a number of fronts. But Tata Tea struggled to put in place the financing required for the acquisition. Not surprising, because this was the first instance of an Indian company attempting to acquire such a large global brand.

Meanwhile, a management team, backed by venture capitalists and entrepreneur Leon Allen, was also keenly pursuing the acquisition of Tetley. They pulled ahead of Tata Tea by quickly arranging the funds required. In June 1995, Allied Domecq announced the sale of the Tetley tea business to this venture capital team. Tata Tea had come so close to achieving its global dream, but had unfortunately fallen short.

KK recalled that moment in London: 'We felt sad. We could not achieve certainty on our financial plan, so our offer had been rejected. But we realized that we had to get our act together on our funding arrangements if we ever desired to make such a large global acquisition. It was a lesson well learnt.'

Despite this deep disappointment, KK kept his eyes on Tetley because he felt that the venture capital firms which had bought the brand would sell their stake in the company at some point in time. And the day came sooner than expected. In February 1999, KK received a call from the global consulting firm Arthur Andersen. 'The owners of Tetley are willing to sell. Would Tata Tea be interested?'

KK quickly spoke to Ratan Tata and Noshir Soonawala at the Tata Group headquarters. They reviewed and agreed on the logic behind acquiring Tetley—a giant leap on to the global canvas, a one-time opportunity to acquire a global tea brand, and a raft of potential synergies in tea sourcing, supply chain and entry into new geographies. In June 1999, in the stately wood-panelled boardroom at Bombay House, the board of directors of Tata Tea, chaired by Ratan Tata, gave its go-ahead. A marble bust of the group's founder, Jamsetji Tata, stands at one end of this boardroom. On that day, I think he may have secretly smiled.

The Tata Tea team went back to London to verify that the business was in good health—to do the due diligence. I was a member of that team and the eyes of the Tetley management were constantly upon us. We had to work with absolute transparency and we did. I think we built a good rapport with them too. On Christmas Eve, 1999, Ken Pringle, the CEO of Tetley, unexpectedly dropped by to meet us and gifted us quaint ceramic figures of the 'Tetley Tea Folk'—warm, animated characters—which I have preserved until today.

In the meantime, KK had learnt his lessons from the failed bid of 1995 and was investing his time and effort to gather the funds required. Eventually, in a long and decisive meeting with Rabobank, he convinced the vice chairman of the bank at that time, Wouter J. Kolff, to provide the financial backing. KK recalls that Kolff finally stood up, looked him in the eye for a few seconds, and said, 'Done!'

Noshir Soonawala, finance director at Tata Sons, helped develop the financial structuring of the transaction. Known to possess a razor-sharp intellect, he put together the required framework for a leveraged buyout, which enabled Tata Tea, a relatively small company, to undertake this massive acquisition. Such a buyout was unheard of in India at that time. In January 2000, after extensive analysis and discussions, a final bid for Tetley, fully backed by financing, was submitted. The bid figure—GBP 271 million (approx. $432 million).

This bid was evaluated by the owners, and, in February 2000, it was finally accepted. Tetley had entered the Tata fold! Tata Group chairman, Ratan Tata, called it a momentous occasion for the company. Indeed, Tata Tea had created history by acquiring a global brand and business several times its size. It had created history for itself, for the Tata Group and for India.

The Tetley acquisition was a path-breaking venture in so many ways and it signalled a new self-belief in India. But here is something I would like to point out. This acquisition took ten long years to fructify, from dream to finish, with many small steps that built trust and confidence, and a deep disappointment along the way that became an opportunity to learn. Each of us can hope to achieve our own audacious dreams if we persist, and learn, and persist.

12

Diamonds, Steel and Hearts of Gold

The Jagersfontein Mine, located in South Africa, is one of the great diamond mines of the world. Discovered in 1870, it yielded over 9.6 million carats of beautiful diamonds over its lifetime. Yet, the unique stone that was discovered here in 1895 was particularly special in more ways than one.

First and foremost, this magnificent large diamond, weighing 245.35 carats, turned out to be the sixth-largest in the world. This means it was twice as large as the legendary Kohinoor. Second, it was a diamond of exceptional purity and sparkle and often described as the most perfectly cut of all large diamonds. But most importantly, as this interesting story will soon reveal to you, it went on to play a very important role for the Tata Group, well beyond the normal remit of diamonds and jewellery.

The large, rough stone was sent to Amsterdam in 1896 for polishing, where it became clear that it would yield a superb, colourless, cushion-cut diamond. A stone so perfect in cut that it could be balanced on its narrow culet, less than 2 mm across. In 1897, it was named the 'Jubilee' diamond to commemorate the diamond jubilee of Queen Victoria. This was a rare instance of a diamond being named for a diamond jubilee, quite a literal commemoration! Indeed, the consortium of three London merchants who owned it then may have even thought that this diamond would be best placed in Her Majesty's royal crown.

However, destiny had other plans in store for the Jubilee diamond. In 1900, it was displayed at the Paris Exposition, which was held to celebrate the achievements of the past hundred years, and also to welcome the new century. The diamond was a centre of attraction at this global fair and received a lot of praise from experts. At that time, it must have caught the imagination of Sir Dorabji Tata, the elder son of Jamsetji Tata, founder of the Tata Group. Two years earlier—on Valentine's Day, 1898—Sir Dorabji Tata had married Meherbai. He was deeply in love with her and he decided to gift her the Jubilee diamond.

Dorabji bought the diamond from the London merchants for around 1,00,000 pounds. Lady Meherbai Tata had it set on a platinum claw and hung on a platinum chain which she could wear around her neck—but only on special occasions. And it is quite possible that she may even have worn it while meeting the then US President Calvin Coolidge or the king and queen of England.

Lady Meherbai Tata was a pioneer of the women's movement in India, and she was also very proud of her Indian roots, so she inevitably wore a saree to celebrate her Indian heritage even while travelling abroad. The Jubilee diamond must have been a perfect accessory complementing her beautiful Parsee sarees. However, this was a very valuable diamond and therefore heavily insured. Dinsi Gazdar, who was a well-known jeweller those days at the Taj Mahal Hotel, Mumbai, remembered Sir Dorabji Tata stating that every time his wife took the diamond out of their safe deposit vault in London, he was 'fined' 200 pounds by the insurance company.

Meanwhile, Sir Dorabji Tata had succeeded his father as chairman of the Tata Group and was busy managing the affairs of Tata Steel, the Taj Mahal Hotel and other business ventures of the group. Tata Steel, based in Jamshedpur, had just undertaken an expansion programme post World War I when the company, which was still in its early years, ran into a host of difficulties ranging from price inflation to labour issues. Demand in Japan, a large market, came spiralling down because of an earthquake there. By 1923, there was a shortage of cash and liquidity, and the Tatas held on for dear life, making valiant efforts to raise funds.

In 1924, a telegram arrived from Jamshedpur bearing ill news. It simply said that there was not enough money left to pay wages to the employees of Tata Steel. Would the fledgling company survive or would it be forced to shut down? Would the dreams and visions that guided the establishment of India's first integrated steel plant come tumbling down?

Sir Dorabji Tata did not hesitate for a moment. He had to save the company so that it could survive the difficult times of that period. His wife, Meherbai, and he decided to pledge their entire personal wealth, which came to around Rs 1 crore (a huge amount in those days), to Imperial Bank to raise funds for Tata Steel. This included all the jewellery owned by his wife, including the Jubilee diamond.

Imperial Bank provided the Tatas with a loan of Rs 1 crore against this personal pledge. That money was used to fund Tata Steel. Soon, the company's expanded production facilities began delivering returns and the situation started to take a turn for the better. Not a single worker was retrenched during the period of intense struggle but shareholders were not paid dividends for the next several years. The company returned to profitability within a few years and the pledge was repaid. By the late 1930s, Tata Steel began to prosper again. By then, Sir Dorabji Tata had passed away, but the personal sacrifice made by him and by his wife, by pledging their wealth and jewellery, had saved Tata Steel from collapse.

In 1931, Lady Meherbai Tata died of leukaemia at the relatively young age of fifty. Sir Dorabji Tata passed away just a year later, in 1932. He had willed his entire fortune to the Sir Dorabji Tata Charitable Trust—including, of course, the Jubilee diamond. The Jubilee diamond was sold through Cartier in the year 1937 and the funds from this sale went to the Trust.

The Sir Dorabji Tata Trust used these funds to establish the Tata Memorial Hospital and many other institutions including the Tata Institute of Social Sciences and the Tata Institute of Fundamental Research. Indeed, this makes the Jubilee diamond unique—it is perhaps the only diamond in the history of mankind that has saved a steel company from collapse, protecting many livelihoods, and has then gone on to birth a cancer hospital as well. No diamond has served worthier causes, and this was only possible because of two wonderful hearts of gold.

But whatever happened to the Jubilee diamond? It was acquired from Cartier by M. Paul-Louis Weiller, a French industrialist. It has since been bought by Robert Mouawad of the House Mouawad, reputed jewellers and watchmakers since 1890. There it rests today, its brilliance as splendid, bright and beguiling as ever, evoking its rich and eventful history. A beautiful, magnificent diamond with a Tata history.

When Sir Dorabji Tata died, the *Times of India* wrote, on 4 June 1932:

Sir Dorabji's fame, however, will not rest on his great (industrial) achievements, splendid as they were, or on his wealth, but it will rest solidly on the use he has made of his possessions.

Truly, what use we put our possessions to is the real value that they serve. The story of the Jubilee diamond stands testimony to this truth.

13

The Slimmest Watch in the Universe

B.G. Dwarakanath (fondly called BGD) is a long-time Tata veteran, having worked for three decades with the Titan Company. He is a restless horologist, technologist and expert photographer with an earthy sense of humour.

In 1997, BGD and his colleague Subramanya Bhat decided to meet Xerxes Desai, the legendary managing director of Titan. They wanted to discuss an audacious project with him, one that no other Indian company had ever undertaken before.

They walked into Desai's sixth-floor corner office at the Titan headquarters in Bangalore. BGD wasted no time in putting forward his proposal.

'We would like to manufacture the slimmest watch movement in the world,' BGD told Xerxes Desai, 'a movement as slim as a credit card. Just 1.15 mm thin, including the battery. A movement which is robust, and can be mass manufactured for use in beautiful, ultra-slim wristwatches. First time, anywhere in the world.'

A movement is the engine inside every watch that keeps it moving and tells the time accurately. Both Desai and BGD knew that slim movements were extremely rare because they were so challenging to design and manufacture. Even the few ultra-slim European and Japanese movements which existed then were produced in very small quantities. The few were very expensive, and in some cases their reliability was in question, and therefore they were virtually museum pieces.

BGD looked at Desai expectantly. 'Sir, this will be a real breakthrough for us, something that is world-class and beyond.' He saw that Desai was looking at him carefully. His eyes had widened; there was absolute silence.

Finally, Desai spoke, in his polished, soft Oxford accent. 'Go ahead.'

BGD and Bhat rushed out of Desai's room. Their hearts were jumping with joy. Their leader was willing to take this risk, invest in something that had never been done before. While they had indeed designed a slim watch movement a few years earlier, which had also won an award in 1996, the proposed ultra-slim 1.15 mm movement would be in another league altogether.

A project team was quickly constituted, including technologists, manufacturing experts and designers. BGD insisted that the team should have the best minds and not people who could be spared for a project which was in the domain of wishful thinking.

'I want each of you to be part of this huge success story,' he told team members. They were excited, but also apprehensive. Most importantly, they were eager and restless.

This was the beginning of the search for many answers. The first big question was: How does one develop such a slim movement with high time-telling accuracy? This would require a step motor with high torque, yet low electric power consumption. The team resolved this challenge by working with

Audemar, a Swiss company, and then married the step motor to an in-house-developed circuit board which was equally thin. Later, the step motor was quickly indigenized by the team with even better performance.

Then, it was important to ensure a long battery life. No one wants to change a watch battery often. To ensure this, the entire internal mechanism had to draw very little current. All parts had to be miniaturized with strict tolerances. Here, again, the technical team worked relentlessly in their laboratories. Eventually, what they achieved was marvellous. The electric power required to light up a 40 watt light bulb for just one hour can power this ultra-slim watch for more than fifty years!

By the year 2000, a working movement was ready. The initial proposal was to sell this ultra-slim movement to Swiss watchmakers, but the Swiss refused outright to buy an Indian watch movement. BGD recalls how a Swiss representative of the famous brand Raymond Weil once told him at the Basel global watch fair that an Indian movement would dilute their strong brand image so the Swiss would never consider using it.

BGD came out of that meeting crestfallen but determined. He had great pride in what his team had developed in India and so did his boss, Xerxes Desai. Once they were back in India, Desai decided that if the Swiss were unwilling to buy the movement, Titan would use it to launch its own branded ultra-slim watch.

Once again, this was a bold decision because there was no consumer research that Indians had any need for ultra-slim watches on their wrists. But that is what courageous marketers do. When they have a breakthrough product, they don't rely on research. Instead, they work to create desire and demand for it.

However, Desai also quickly jolted the team into the reality of what this decision meant.

'Our ultra-slim watch has to be made for Indian consumers to wear every day. So it has to be water resistant,' he told the team, 'otherwise it cannot survive Indian conditions. This is essential.'

Once again, BGD and his team went into a huddle. Here was a new challenge. How could such a slim movement and a watch with such thin surfaces be made water-resistant?

This would require the watch to be housed in an external case which had very thin walls but was extremely strong and robust. Here again, BGD, along with his colleague B.V. Nagaraj, approached Swiss manufacturers who were most experienced in the world of watches. Once again, the Swiss said 'no' and shut the door on them. Swiss factories were unwilling to accept this challenge or help Titan. Would this now spell the end of the project?

Of course not—because the Titan team was unwilling to give up on their cherished dream. BGD recalls that the team came together and decided that if the Swiss would not help, they would do it themselves, back home in India, in their own beloved Titan watch factory at Hosur in Tamil Nadu. We will open the eyes of the world to what we can do by ourselves, the team determined. When that sort of spirit comes alive, all impediments melt away.

And the challenges did melt away. After several iterations, the external case and a watch with the required water resistance up to a depth of 30 metres was created by Titan. The team decided to use a sapphire crystal on the watch rather than glass, which would get shattered if it were to be ground to such slim dimensions. And then, the team used the technique of all-round fitting on the back cover of the watch so that it could be easily opened for servicing and battery replacement. Vinay Kamath's excellent book on Titan contains many more interesting details of this challenging product development journey.

Meanwhile, Michael Foley, the lead appearance parts designer on the project, was working closely with Xerxes Desai to finalize the aesthetics of the watch. 'I was excited by the prospect of creating a watch that was virtually invisible,' says Michael. He adds, 'We wanted the watch to celebrate the ultra-slim movement inside, to feel as thin as an edge, and not really a surface.'

To celebrate this beautiful design philosophy, the unique watch was named the 'Titan Edge'. What a perfect name. Not just a watch which looked like the thin edge of something but a horological marvel which was at the cutting edge of technological excellence.

The entire watch, including the internal movement and external case, was just 3.5 mm thin, and feather-light at just around 14 grams in weight. The slimmest commercially available watch in the universe, and perhaps amongst the lightest watches too. It was priced affordably as well because Titan had manufactured this product at a fraction of what it would have cost to make in Switzerland.

The Titan Edge was launched in Bangalore in May 2002. In the launch advertising, the watch was shown sideways to emphasize its slimness. Since then, many new designs have been introduced. The Edge has been a huge and enduring success in India and several other countries. Most recently, a ceramic version of the Edge has been launched, which is the slimmest ceramic watch in the world. The Edge has also been recognized as one of the finest product innovations to come out of post-Independence India.

That's why lakhs of Indians wear the Titan Edge with pride. Not merely because it is so sleek and beautiful, but also because it is a technological marvel made in India, which the entire world envies today.

BGD, the man who had been rebuffed repeatedly by the Swiss earlier, recalls that he wore the Titan Edge to the Basel watch fair in a subsequent year. There, he met the grand old man of Swiss watches, Nicolas Hayek Sr, chairman of the Swatch Group, on the sidelines of a media event. He showed Hayek the Titan Edge with pride. Hayek was struck by the slimness of the watch; he held BGD's hands for a long time and kept peering at the watch. He had it photographed. And then, he turned around to BGD, and said, 'Amazing!'

BGD attributes the outstanding success of the Edge to the wonderful team that came together for this project. And to the leadership of Titan, which ensured that the team worked freely, without any fear of failure.

An Indian company of the Tata Group, Titan, had delivered what seemed impossible through their sheer tenacity. This was truly 'Make in India' at its very best. Technology, design, belief and persistence had come together to create a product which is today ranked among the most iconic watches in the world.

When we believe, we make it happen.

14

Coffee, Tea and J.R.D.

J.R.D. Tata was the founder of Tata Airlines, which went on to become Air India. Way back in the 1940s and 1950s, this airline was the first Indian global entity, proudly taking the Indian flag to international skies. In 1948, Air India inaugurated its first international service, from Mumbai to London, a proud moment for the country.

J.R.D. was determined to make Air India the best airline in the world, notwithstanding the fierce competition from a host of other global airlines. For him, this was essential, because Air India was not just an airline, but a proud carrier of India's image across the world. During the inaugural international flight, on which he also flew, he watched carefully for the reactions of passengers, and was greatly relieved when everything went very well, including landing in London right on time. He said, 'It was for me a great and stirring event . . . seeing the Indian flag displayed on both sides of the Malabar Princess [the name of that particular aircraft] as she stood proudly on the apron at the airports of Cairo, Geneva and London filled me with joy and emotion.'

Thereafter, he was obsessed with making the airline special, and he knew that this required the highest standards of customer service and excellence. He told the airline's employees, 'I want that the passengers who travel with us do not have occasion to complain. I want to establish that there is no airline which is better liked by passengers, that is safer and more punctual, where the food and service is better, and which sets a better image than Air India.'

As early as 1949, with constant attention to every small detail, these aspirations were coming true. In fact, the prime minister of India, Pandit Jawaharlal Nehru, wrote to J.R.D. Tata on 7 May 1949, specifically complimenting him on the high quality offered by the airline. Nehru wrote: 'This is just a brief letter to express my great appreciation of the quality of the Air India International Service. I have now travelled on four occasions between India and England in it, and the more experience I have had of it, the better I like it. I think that Air India International has played not an unimportant part in raising the prestige of India abroad . . . So, congratulations.'

Air India soon became legendary for its punctuality. Legend has it that people in Geneva, in those years, could set their watches to the time at which the Air India flight flew over their city. In those initial days, J.R.D. would fly one of the aircraft himself once every fifteen days. During these flights, he would insist on such high standards of accuracy that other pilots tried to dodge flying with him. The historian R.M. Lala tells us that on one such flight, J.R.D. asked his co-pilot, Capt. Visvanath, for the ground speed. '145 miles per hour,' replied Visvanath. J.R.D. was not satisfied. He took out his slide rule, worked out his own calculations, and responded, 'It's 145.5.' Those were the standards of accuracy he expected if the airline was to keep perfect time.

J.R.D. Tata's blue notes were extraordinary in their attention to detail and relentless push for excellence in all matters big and small. After every Air India flight that he took, he would send these 'blue notes' to the management, summarizing his observations, including encouraging comments and scathing criticism. Here are some extracts from his notes in the year 1951, after he had flown Air India to Europe and back home: 'Chairs: I found on VT-DAR that some of the seats recline much more than the others. As a result, those seats are more comfortable. I suggest that all our seats be adjusted for a maximum reclining angle, except, of course, the rearmost seats which are limited by bulkheads.'

And even more interesting is this note: 'The tea served on board from Geneva is, without exaggeration, indistinguishable in colour from coffee . . . I do not know whether the black colour of the tea is due to the quality (of tea leaves) used or due to excessive brewing. I suggest that the Station Manager at Geneva be asked to look into the matter.'

Because of such meticulous attention to detail and excellence, Air India topped the list of airlines in the world in 1968 as per a survey done by the *Daily Mail*, London. In fact, in that same year, 75 per cent of Air India's passengers were foreigners who came from countries with their own airlines. I have also heard that when Singapore wanted to launch an airline (now it is famous as Singapore Airlines), Prime Minister Lee Kuan Yew advised his team to study the high standards that had been set by Air India.

Ratan Tata, writing in a beautiful commemorative book where many Air Indians have offered tributes to J.R.D. Tata, has said of him:

Many of us who knew Jeh [J.R.D. Tata] intimately knew that Air India was as important to him as the industrial empire he headed. While he led the Tata empire with distinction, Air India was his personal creation and personal passion. He built it and it became the airline recognised by many international carriers as the gold standards of service. No other enterprise in the country enjoyed that type of international recognition. His personal quest for excellence, his attention to detail and his ability to keep abreast of new technologies relating to aviation and the airline business, provided the leadership that made Air India an airline of choice, and gave it true global stature.

In my office, for the past three decades, stands a quote from J.R.D. Tata, which guided his own actions, and which inspires me every single day. He said: 'One must forever strive for excellence, or even perfection, in any task however small, and never be satisfied with the second best.' Remember, for instance, his note on tea and coffee.

15

Tata Institute of Fundamental Research

On 19 August 1943, a young scientist, in his early thirties, wrote to J.R.D. Tata. He said, 'The lack of proper conditions and intelligent financial support hampers the development of science in India, at the pace at which the talent in the country would warrant.' He then pointed out that for Indian science to progress, far greater financial support was essential, particularly for pure and fundamental scientific research which would only provide economic returns in the long term.

This young scientist went on to mention that he had received job offers from Cambridge and Princeton after the end of World War II, but he felt that 'it is one's duty to stay in one's own country' and help in creating new institutions for national progress. He then put forward a proposal to build a school of physics, comparable to the best in the world, and sought support from the Tata Group.

The scientist who wrote this letter was Dr Homi J. Bhabha, known today as the father of India's atomic energy programme.

Interestingly, he was also a nephew of feminist icon Lady Meherbai Tata whose story is briefly chronicled elsewhere in this book. J.R.D. Tata responded to him promptly and with great encouragement: 'If you and some of your colleagues in the scientific world will put up concrete proposals backed by a sound case, I think there is a very good chance that the Tata Trusts would respond.'

Greatly motivated by J.R.D. Tata's response, Dr Bhabha quickly submitted, in 1944, a formal proposal to the Sir Dorabji Tata Trust, for establishment of a centre of excellence in physics and mathematics. Writing to the chairman of the Trust, on 12 March 1944, he stated, with great foresight, that such an institute would ensure that India had its own expertise for the development of nuclear energy in the future, and would not have to look abroad for it. It is fascinating that he said this more than a year before the first atomic bomb exploded in 1945, and well before the world woke up to the power of nuclear energy.

Dr Bhabha went on to say in his detailed proposal, which is testimony to his vision:

> I do not think that anyone acquainted with scientific development in other countries would deny the need in India for such a school as I propose . . . The scheme I am now submitting to you is but an embryo from which I hope to build up in the course of time a school of physics comparable with the best anywhere . . . If Tatas would decide to sponsor an Institute such as I propose through their Trusts, I am sure that they would be taking the initiative in a move which will be supported soon from many directions, and be of lasting benefit to India.

Dr Bhabha's proposal also received complete support from Prof. A.V. Hill, who had won the Nobel Prize in 1922, and was then senior secretary of the Royal Society. The Sir Dorabji Tata Trust, named in honour of the second chairman of the Tata Group, duly considered this proposal in light of its own policy, which included fostering new institutions that would serve major social objectives. The trustees saw how the vision of Dr Bhabha would immensely benefit the country, and decided to support him in the creation of the Tata Institute of Fundamental Research (TIFR).

TIFR opened its doors in 1945, initially for a brief while in Bangalore, but shifted to Mumbai soon thereafter. Its first Mumbai home was a bungalow called 'Kenilworth', located on Pedder Road. The Cosmic Ray Group was the first scientific team to begin functioning, followed by the Nuclear Emulsion and Electron Magnetism Group. The computer science and technology team began its work in 1954, and a full-scale computer, named the TIFRAC, was commissioned in 1960. TIFRAC (an acronym for Tata Institute of Fundamental Research Automatic Calculator) was the first Indian-made digital computer, a proud moment for the country.

In 1962, TIFR moved to its beautiful new campus in Colaba, Mumbai, where it stands even today. When India began its atomic energy programme in the 1960s, TIFR had already trained competent scientists to steer this important national effort. In fact, when 'Apsara', the first atomic reactor in Asia and India, was built, its control systems were constructed under the auspices of this institute.

From the beginning, the central and state governments were included in this important venture, which addressed the sensitive subject of nuclear energy. In 1955, the Union government took responsibility for this institute, with the Tatas continuing to be present on its governing council. Today, TIFR is a national centre of the Government of India under the purview of the Department of Atomic Energy.

TIFR has passionately pursued the vision of Dr Homi Bhabha in creating a world-class research centre. Apart from its pioneering contribution to India's atomic energy programme, and the building of India's first digital computer, it has many other significant achievements to its credit. It helped discover the farthest radio galaxy. It discovered atmospheric neutrinos. Scientists here showed that smell and taste are genetically coded. It discovered nanodomains on cell membranes. It pursues cutting-edge astronomical research and continues to embark on new frontiers for tomorrow's India.

India's first prime minister, Jawaharlal Nehru, laid the foundation stone for the new TIFR campus in 1953. Paying tribute to the Tatas for the advancement of science in India, he said, 'They have a vision to look ahead without the profit motive. I might add a word of appreciation of the tradition of Tatas for their pioneering spirit in formulating such beneficial schemes.'

TIFR still has the stamp of the man who started it all, Dr Homi Bhabha. In 1966, just four years after TIFR had moved to its new home, this great son of India passed away tragically, in an air crash in the Swiss Alps. He was on his way to attend a scientific conference in Vienna, and was only fifty-five years old. India's atomic energy programme, as well as TIFR, stands testimony to the outstanding contributions made by this versatile genius within his relatively short lifespan.

16

The Legend of Charles Page Perin

Jamsetji Tata, founder of the Tata Group, dreamt of a huge, modern steel plant for India way back in the 1880s. He was convinced that steel was essential for the development of his beloved country—for the building of railways, buildings, bridges and other important infrastructure. Given his keen interest in this subject, he kept a book full of newspaper cuttings on the mineral resources of India with every detail of where they could be found.

Most people were sceptical of his dream. Famously, Sir Frederick Upcott, at that time the chief commissioner for the Indian Railways, is reported to have sneered at this enterprise by saying, 'Do you mean to say that Tatas propose to make steel rails to British specifications? Why, I will undertake to eat every pound of steel rail they succeed in making.'

But Jamsetji Tata was a determined and persuasive man. He met the British Secretary of State for India, Lord George Hamilton, in the year 1902, and managed to convince him that a steel plant would be very useful for the development of the country. But now a big question faced him—from where would he obtain the expertise required for the manufacture of steel? India did not possess the capability, so Jamsetji decided that he would bring the world's best expertise to the country. In his heart of hearts, he would have known that it was no easy task to attract the foremost global technologists to the heartlands of an underdeveloped nation.

That hardly deterred him in his vision for India. He set sail for the USA, home to the world's finest iron and steel industry at the time, in September 1902. Eventually, after surveying Alabama, Chattanooga and Chicago, he reached Pittsburgh, famous for its iron and steel industry. There, he met Julian Kennedy, one of the world's foremost metallurgical engineers of that time.

Julian Kennedy listened to Jamsetji Tata's scheme, warned him that this was a costly project, and then suggested that the person most qualified to help him undertake the geological work required to start a steel plant in India was Charles Page Perin, an eminent consulting engineer in New York. Jamsetji immediately travelled to New York, where Perin had a flourishing practice. He was set on meeting him and attracting him to India, however difficult this task should prove to be.

To see what happened next, we read the notes of Charles Page Perin, who vividly described his first encounter with Jamsetji Tata:

> I was poring over some accounts in the office when the door opened, and a stranger in a strange garb entered. He walked in, leaned over my desk, and looked at me fully a minute in silence. Finally, he said in a deep voice, 'Are you Charles Page Perin ?' I said, 'Yes.' He stared at me again silently for a

long time. Then he slowly said: 'I believe I have found the man I have been looking for. Julian Kennedy has written to you that I am going to build a steel plant in India. I want you to come to India with me, to find suitable iron ore and coking coal and the necessary fluxes. I want you to take charge as my consulting engineer. Mr Kennedy will build the steel plant wherever you advise, and I will foot the bill. Will you come to India with me?'

I was dumbfounded, naturally. But you don't know what character and force radiated from Tata's face. And kindliness, too. 'Well,' I said, 'yes, I will go.' And I did.

I have reflected on this remarkable story so many times. An unknown Indian merchant attracting the world's best consulting engineer from the great city of New York to the jungles of eastern India to set up a steel plant in an unknown location, all in his very first encounter. That strength of character and force which radiated from Jamsetji Tata's face so powerfully and magnetically that morning could only have come from his abiding love for his country. When you love your country so dearly that you are willing to go around the world searching for the keys to its development, when you are willing to set aside your riches to work unconditionally for its progress, then, I say, the world falls at your feet. There is no greater force on the face of this earth.

Charles Page Perin came to India. Inspired by Jamsetji Tata, he worked most willingly in places as far-flung as the Dhalli and Rajhara hills. He helped Jamsetji Tata and his sons establish Tata Steel at Sakchi, which was later renamed Jamshedpur. When the company faced some initial difficulties with its open-hearth furnaces, Perin helped resolve these problems too. On 16 February 1912, the first ingot of steel successfully rolled out of the Tata plant. It was steel of the finest quality. In fact, during

World War I, Tata Steel supplied significant quantities of steel to help in the Allied war effort.

By that time, Jamsetji Tata had already passed away. His son, Dorabji Tata, recalled the British chief commissioner's sneering statement, and is reported to have said that if Sir Frederick Upcott had carried out his undertaking, he would have had some 'slight indigestion'. Today, more than a century later, Tata Steel stands proud, as one of the finest steel companies the world has ever known.

There is an interesting footnote to this story. Perin's wife also accompanied him to India later, perhaps encouraged by his description of his new boss, Jamsetji Tata. She was very keen on education. So, to pay tribute to her memory, the first school in Jamshedpur was established in 1915 and named in her honour as the Mrs Keoke Monroe Perin Memorial (KMPM) School. Today, Jamshedpur is among the cities with the highest literacy rates in India.

17

The Fight against Cancer

In the Parel area of Mumbai stands an institution which all of us in India should be proud of. It has touched the lives of lakhs of people by helping them fight the scourge of cancer. Over 64,000 patients visit it every year. Moreover, 70 per cent of all patients who are treated here receive treatment free of charge. When a patient recovers from cancer and goes back home to his family, back to a healthy and happy life, that is the moment when doctors at this hospital feel most fulfilled. Because that is truly the work of God.

Here is the story of the Tata Memorial Hospital and how it took birth. Today, and over the past several decades, the hospital has been supported and managed by the Department of Atomic Energy. In 1941, when it was founded, it was yet another pioneering effort by the Tata Group, a gift to a nation which did not have a comprehensive cancer hospital of its own.

Sir Dorabji Tata, the second chairman of the Tata Group, was determined to establish in India a facility for the treatment of cancer. In 1932, his wife, Lady Meherbai Tata, had sadly died of leukaemia. Shortly thereafter, Sir Dorabji Tata also passed away. But such was his determination and commitment to the cause that the trustees of the Sir Dorabji Tata Trust immediately took upon themselves the project of creating for India its first cancer hospital.

The Tata Group, which was headed by Sir Nowroji Saklatvala at that time, reached out to the American cancer specialist Dr John Spies, and invited him to visit India. Dr Spies came to India, studied the situation, and recommended setting up a comprehensive hospital where all effective methods of cancer treatment would be available at one place. But that was easier said than done. This was the time of the deep economic depression of the 1930s. There was great doubt about whether the Sir Dorabji Tata Trust could support such an ambitious and expensive venture.

Eventually, in the creation of all great institutions, there comes a moment when vision overcomes doubt and forges the way ahead. J.R.D. Tata played an active role in forging this vision, and the Trust firmly decided that it would overcome all odds and establish Asia's first comprehensive cancer hospital that would carry out the triple objectives of treatment, research and education. Construction of the Tata Memorial Hospital began in 1937, in the vicinity of the Haffkine Institute in Mumbai. At the same time, Indian doctors were sent abroad to modern clinics in Europe and the USA for specialized training.

This was an incredibly difficult venture. Dr Clifford Manshardt, who was closely connected with this project, said later: 'Only those who were associated with the hospital project during the years of its planning know the amount of hard work that went into the making of the Tata Memorial Hospital. An undertaking of the magnitude of the Tata Memorial Hospital would have been difficult in any country. But to rear an institution of this kind, in the face of the limitations under which we were working in Bombay, required imagination, energy, patience, pertinacity and obstinacy.'

Despite the economic depression, and the outbreak of World War II, both of which could have derailed this project, the Tata Group forged ahead. Such determination and resilience in conditions of adversity are the hallmarks of pioneers. The Tata Trusts made a capital grant of Rs 30 lakh, a huge sum in those days, to fund the hospital. In 1941, the hospital was completed, and was inaugurated by the governor of Bombay, Sir Roger Lumley. The facility included operating theatres, research laboratories and lecture rooms. The departments of surgery, pathology, radiology, radiophysics and anaesthesia were also in place. Except for two American surgeons, all the staff were entirely and proudly Indian. This was the first such comprehensive cancer hospital not just in India, but in the whole of Asia.

The Tata Trusts continued funding the hospital entirely until 1949, after which grants were also received from the Government of India. In 1957, the hospital was handed over to the Government of India, and since 1962, it has been admirably managed by the Department of Atomic Energy.

In recent years, the Tata Trusts have continued the fight against cancer with admirable energy, under the determined leadership of Ratan Tata. In 2012, the Tata Medical Centre was established in Kolkata to address the lack of suitable facilities in eastern India. Tata Trusts are also setting up cancer research and treatment centres in Varanasi, Tirupati, Bhubaneswar, Ranchi, Allahabad and Mangalore. The trusts are also partnering state governments in building statewise cancer facility networks in Assam, Odisha, Jharkhand, Telangana and Nagaland. This is an important fight against a terrible disease across our nation.

In so many ways, therefore, the words of Sir Roger Lumley, at the inauguration of the Tata Memorial Hospital in 1941, continue to echo into the future. He said that although the House of Tata was already well known for its philanthropic projects, 'none would attain a greater importance, or reflect greater credit on its founders, than the Tata Memorial Hospital for cancer'.

Take a moment and think about any of your colleagues, friends, relatives or acquaintances who have had to fight cancer. And reflect on the Tata Memorial Hospital, which has led this fight in India, with exceptional patient care and research, for over seventy-five years now.

18

Memorable Letter to a Schoolteacher

In the year 1965, J.R.D. Tata received a letter from a schoolteacher in Kolkata named K.C. Bhansali. His response to Bhansali is not just memorable but one that each of us can cherish. Here is the story of this letter and why it is so extraordinary.

K.C. Bhansali, in his letter dated 6 August 1965, inquired of J.R.D. Tata about the guiding principles of his life. This educationist lived in Howrah and he was keen to understand the principles which had governed J.R.D.'s life, which had already made a huge impact on the country by then.

In 1965, when J.R.D. received this letter, he was sixty-one years of age. It was now twenty-seven years since he had assumed charge as chairman of the Tata Group. By then, he had already given the country its first commercial airline, Tata Airlines (now Air India). He had guided the establishment of Tata Motors, then called TELCO. He had given India the Bombay Plan, the country's first comprehensive economic plan, along with three other prominent industrialists.

The Tata Memorial Hospital and the Tata Institute of Fundamental Research, two iconic national institutions, had been established during his tenure as chairman. And this was just the tip of the iceberg.

As chairman of the Tata Group and of several companies, J.R.D. would no doubt have been caught up in a busy schedule. It would perhaps have been simple to ignore the schoolteacher's letter or request one of his officers to send him a brief response out of courtesy. Instead, J.R.D. Tata took the time and effort to craft out a detailed and thoughtful response. Here is the extraordinary letter that he wrote to Bhansali on 13 September 1965:

Dear Mr Bhansali,

I thank you for your letter of the 6th August, enquiring what have been the guiding principles which have kindled my path and my career. I do not consider myself to be an 'illustrious personality', but only an ordinary businessman and citizen who has tried to make the best of his opportunities to advance the cause of India's industrial and economic development. Any such guiding principles I might unconsciously have had in my life can be summarized as follows:

That nothing worthwhile is ever achieved without deep thought and hard work;

That one must think for oneself and never accept at their face value slogans and catch phrases to which, unfortunately, our people are too easily susceptible;

That one must forever strive for excellence, or even perfection, in any task however small, and never be satisfied with the second best;

That no success or achievement in material terms is worthwhile, unless it serves the needs or interests of the country and its people, and is achieved by fair and honest means;

That good human relations not only bring great personal rewards but are essential to the success of any enterprise.

Yours sincerely,

J.R.D. Tata

I have found this letter extraordinary because it is so simple and yet so powerful.

In less than 200 words, J.R.D. Tata had put forward the guiding principles by which he lived his life. When I first read this brief letter, it brought to my mind President Abraham Lincoln's famous Gettysburg Address, which was less than 275 words in length. The most powerful ideas are inevitably communicated in such compact and brief pieces of communication. They do not need lengthy documents or orations.

The letter is very thoughtfully crafted because it puts forward five independent principles which are enmeshed with each other in the creation of a good, successful and fulfilling life—hard work, thoughtfulness, excellence, ethical behaviour, good human relations and patriotism. J.R.D. has drawn these excellent principles not from any fancy theoretical construct but also from his own life experiences, which are always the best teacher.

The letter resonates with every reader. In fact, each of these principles is a pointer that we can use in our own lives, wherever we are, and whatever we are engaged in. All of us wish to work hard, and we would like to be thoughtful. Don't we often wish we could push ourselves even more to attain excellence, even perfection, in everything we do? And so many of us aspire to do something impactful for our nation and community, ahead of everything else. It is possible for us to take to heart each of these points, and apply them to our everyday work, whether we are completing a work project, or deciding on how to engage with a colleague.

And, finally, this letter is so simple to understand. It has no traces of management jargon. J.R.D. has written these guiding principles in simple, straightforward yet perfect English, which is a pleasure to read. This is the art of simplicity in communication that we often forget when we get sucked into the jargon and hyperbole of the corporate world. No wonder Edgar F. Kaiser, the American industrialist, said this to J.R.D. Tata in his letter of February 1972: 'I have commented before on your ability to use the English language. I repeat again, I don't know anyone who does it better.'

For more than thirty years now, J.R.D. Tata's guiding principles—an extract from this memorable letter—have stood on my work desk at the Tata Group, printed on a bright, laminated board that also bears his photograph. Whenever I need a special burst of motivation or some internal guidance, I look at these simple, powerful points, and always draw great energy from them.

I think this extraordinary letter, and the principles it sets forth, will stand the test of time.

19

League of Tata Scholars

A common thread connects former president of India K.R. Narayanan, nuclear scientist Dr Raja Ramanna, astrophysicist Prof. J.V. Narlikar and economist Dr V.K.R.V. Rao. A common thread named Tata.

They are all Tata Scholars and recipients of the J.N. Tata Endowment Scholarship, which was the first such scholarship set up specifically for Indians going abroad for higher studies. Amazingly, this scholarship was established way back in 1892 to provide brilliant Indian students a path to the finest universities in the world to enable them to qualify for coveted professions of their choice.

In 1889, Jamsetji Tata, founder of the Tata Group, was deeply inspired by an address delivered by Lord Reay, the governor of Bombay, on the importance of learning and research to the future of India. As Jamsetji reflected on this address, he also became deeply conscious of the deficiencies of higher education in the country. His ambitious plans for the establishment of an Indian university of science would necessarily take time to blossom. So what could he do immediately to catalyse the higher education of Indians?

Jamsetji Tata was a man of action. He decided that he would establish a scholarship scheme to send a few chosen Indian students to England each year for higher education at the best universities there. This was an audacious and pioneering thought for the time because no one had attempted this before. The cost of sending an Indian student abroad was very significant. Jamsetji also decided that this scheme should not have any shades of charity to it, so he decided to provide the funds to the selected students as loans, at a nominal rate of interest. Students could then repay the loan in instalments after they eventually began earning their livelihoods. This also ensured that the scholarship fund was constantly renewed and preserved for the future.

This scheme marked the birth of the J.N. Tata Endowment Scholarship. The very first Tata Scholar was a lady medical doctor, Ms Freany K.R. Cama. In those days, the Tata scholarship loan she received for her studies abroad was Rs 10,000. She returned as one of India's pioneer gynaecologists and rendered great service to her country. Her scholarship agreement, dated 7 April 1892, bears Jamsetji Tata's signature, and documents her desire to pursue in England 'the study of midwifery and the diseases of women and children for a period of two years'.

Then, in 1902, Jamsetji also signed an agreement with a lady called Ms Krishnabai Kelavkar, who went on to qualify for a Fellowship of the Royal College of Surgeons, Dublin. Even in those early days, the higher education of women was clearly a high priority for the founder of the Tata Group.

Jamsetji Tata was keen that many Indians qualify for the Indian administrative and technical services. He wished to see his countrymen in these high echelons of civic responsibility. And opportunity worked wonders, for sure. Many needy students, benefiting from the Tata Scholarships, returned to take up positions of high office. Soon, several members of the Indian Civil Service were Tata Scholars. So were many of India's leading doctors, engineers, educationists and barristers. The seed that Jamsetji had sown was bearing fruit, very quickly.

Jamsetji Tata was very proud of his scholars. His biographer, Frank Harris, quotes Jamsetji as saying: 'Our young men have proved that they can not only hold their own against the best rivals in Europe on the latter's ground, but can beat them hollow.' What an inspiring statement this must have been for young Indians, who were then labouring under the heavy yoke of the British rulers!

Jamsetji went on to say, 'Every Indian that gets into the Civil Service I have calculated effects a saving to this country of two lakhs of rupees: that is what a civilian's pay, allowance and pension come to, most of which usually goes to Britain.' When I read this, I wonder so much about this man and the multiple perspectives through which he thought for his country. For him, it was always 'nation first'.

The list of meritorious Indian students who have received the Tata Scholarships and have pursued their studies abroad is an impressive one. Some names have already been mentioned at the start of this story, including President K.R. Narayanan and scientist Dr Raja Ramanna. Other Tata Scholars include Sir Ardeshir Dalal, ICS; Sir Nowrosji Wadia, famous jurist; Dr Dinanath Rangnekar, editor of the *Economic Times*; Dr Bal D. Tilak, director, National Chemical Laboratory; Mr Yezdi H. Malegam, who headed S.B. Billimoria & Co.; Mr Xerxes Desai, who founded the Titan Company; and Dr Jivraj Mehta, former chief minister of Gujarat and Indian high commissioner to the United Kingdom.

The entire list of Tata Scholars is too long to mention here. Between 1892 and 2018, there have been as many as

5365 recipients of the J.N. Tata Endowment Scholarship. Until today, every single year, meritorious Indian students who wish to study at the best universities in the world—for master's, PhD and postdoctoral studies in any educational stream—can apply for this loan scholarship. To be a Tata Scholar remains a distinction today, as it was over a century ago.

At the heart of the Tata Scholarships is Jamsetji Tata's strong faith in his fellow countrymen. More than 125 years ago, when higher education overseas was inaccessible to most Indians, he wanted to encourage talented young Indians to go out into the wide world, drink from the best fountains of knowledge, and return to serve in the progress of their nation. He had a strong belief that Indians could rank amongst the best in the world, in every field. Yes, he was a patron of learning. But, most of all, he was a champion of his countrymen.

20

The Weavers of Okhai

Okhamandal lies at the tip of the Saurashtra peninsula in Gujarat, the westernmost state of India. Beauty, irony and industry coexist here. This is home to Dwarka, the beautiful temple of Lord Krishna. This is one of the most arid and drought-prone regions of the country. This is also the proud home of Tata Chemicals, the place where Tata Salt, one of India's best-loved brands, is produced with great pride.

From Okhamandal comes this beautiful story of livelihoods and hope for tribal women who now dream of Paris and Milan. This area is a mosaic of many diverse tribes and communities, including the tall, strapping Vaghers and the nomadic Rabaris. Walk with me to the village of Arambdha and meet Ramiben Nagesh, a Rabari woman. Garbed in bright-red tribal attire, she sports large gold earrings and heavy, long neckwear. She talks to us with great pride about Okhai, a fashion brand created by her friends and herself, with help from the Tata Chemicals Society for Rural Development (TCSRD).

Several years ago, Ramiben joined a women's self-help group set up by TCSRD, designed to empower women and help them generate income for themselves. This dry area does not encourage tribal women to take up any careers beyond taking care of their family livestock, so this was a big change. Then, in 2002, she heard about a unique and creative effort that was also being established by the same organization to create and popularize handicrafts from the Okhamandal region under a brand called 'Okhai' (which means 'from Okhamandal').

Ramiben's curiosity was piqued immediately because colour and artwork are all-pervasive in Rabari homes. The walls of their huts are decorated with appliquéd and finely embroidered wall hangings. These walls are repainted immediately after weddings with images of men, women, animals and birds set in striking patterns. Many Rabari designs also incorporate interpretations of Lord Krishna as represented at Dwarka. Like all other Rabari children, Ramiben had been taught art from a very young age by her family elders.

So she felt a rekindling of her creative urges when she heard of Okhai. She enlisted the support of her husband and mother-in-law and joined the Okhai team at Mithapur. In the early days, she worked on pillows, bed sheets and wall decorations. It was fun, and she was paid for her efforts. Then, one fine morning, she was requested to travel to Ahmedabad to meet a fashion designer. She had never left home earlier to traverse such a distance. But the promise of breaking through a fresh knowledge barrier gave her the impetus to do so. Accompanied by a few other Rabari women, she went on this life-changing visit.

There, she met with Rupali Agarwal, a reputed designer from Gujarat. Ramiben listened and saw with great interest the cuts of apparel that appeal to modern women, the design processes involved, and how to maintain the originality of Rabari designs while interpreting them for today. She returned to Mithapur, her head milling with a thousand different design ideas. Here was raw talent and creativity being unlocked and set free!

Ramiben and her colleagues incorporated many of the design expert's inputs as they went about creating lovely kurtas, kurtis, bedcovers, tablecloths, shawls, skirts, aprons and bags. There are special murals that depict village scenes. There is exquisite beadwork, bold embroidery and innovative mirror-work. All these products proudly carry the ethnic designs of Okhamandal that are now interpreted with increasing sophistication and finesse. These are the beautiful fashion garments that now constitute brand Okhai, one of the most original and authentic fashion brands ever to be created in our country. Over the years, Okhai has now come to feature women's apparel, accessories, home decor, and most recently, even masks.

What has this business done for the tribal women of Okhai? Listen to Ramiben speak: 'Looking after goats and cows is fine up to a point, but we need a better future for our children. You need education to do well in today's world. So, I have told my husband, let's use my earnings from Okhai to give our children good schooling and higher education. I myself appeared for my twelfth standard exams recently. My work at Okhai has given me the confidence to study even more. My children are very happy that their mother is also studying, and when I returned from the exam hall, they asked me with a stern expression— Mummy, have you done well in your exams?'

Meet Lakhuben, a Rabari woman who has evolved into an expert master cutter of Okhai garments. In her previous job, she was a manual labourer, cutting and crushing stones for a paltry sum of money. Today, she is a proud part of a fashion brand.

Meet Khatijaben, a senior woman and the sole breadwinner of her family. She confidently handles quality control of the garments and pays for her daughter's education primarily with her earnings from Okhai.

Meet Zareena Kureshi, a young bubbly girl and master cutter of garments, who declares: 'Okhai is my life.' She says Okhai has provided her invaluable training at the National Institute of Fashion Technology, and has opened her eyes to a fresh new world.

Meet 2300 women, all earning their livelihoods from Okhai today: 1500 of these women work in and around Mithapur, and the rest are based in Rajasthan, Babrala and Lucknow. Most of them use their income to educate their children. Today, Okhai enables them to send their girls and boys to study further, including evening tuitions when required.

When I visited Mithapur a few years ago, I asked these tribal weavers of Okhai what their ambition for the brand was. Their response: 'We would like to see our garments on the fashion ramps of Milan.' As I looked at them, I found them looking back at me, smiling at me with twinkling eyes and weaving away. My heart swelled with pride, and I held back a few tears too.

In fact, during the past two years, Okhai has broken new ground and done very successful exhibitions in Paris, Singapore and New York. Today, over 40,000 women customers trust Okhai and purchase its exquisite garments regularly. Customers love the beautiful Okhai designs and craftsmanship, including mirror-work, patchwork and embroidery. They also know that, with every purchase, they are helping rural women become proud wage earners for their families.

The constant goal of the Tata Chemicals team that works with Okhai is to create the next Ramiben, the next Zareena, the next Lakhuben. Because this is the brand of their livelihoods and dreams. India is home to a few other similarly conscious brands today. May a thousand Okhais bloom all around us for the economically backward women of our country.

21

Nani Palkhivala: Brilliant Mind, Remarkable Man

It would not be an exaggeration to say that Nani Ardeshir Palkhivala ranks among the greatest intellectuals of modern India. He joined the Tata Group in 1961, became a director of Tata Sons at the young age of forty-one years, and worked very closely with J.R.D. Tata for over thirty years. He even served as director of Tata Steel, Tata Motors, Indian Hotels and as chairman of Tata Consultancy Services. He was a lawyer, taxation expert, corporate leader, diplomat, an economist and an orator par excellence. But that's only what the world sees him as; who really was this remarkable man? What made him so successful, and what can we learn from him?

The cornerstone of Nani Palkhivala's success was that he was true to his beliefs—a man of absolute intellectual integrity. When Palkhivala was first recruited into the Tata Group, he had been given the dispensation to continue his private legal practice simultaneously. In 1975, he agreed to defend the then prime minister, Indira Gandhi, when the

Allahabad High Court overturned her election to the Lok Sabha on the grounds of corruption. He decided to become her lawyer even if he disagreed with many of her economic policies—only because of his belief that the judiciary should not be permitted to dismiss an elected official on what were, in his view, inadequate legal grounds.

Palkhivala won a stay in Indira Gandhi's favour, but when he heard shortly thereafter that she had declared a state of Emergency, he felt outraged. This was, according to him, a subversion of the Constitution. So, at personal risk to himself, he decided to withdraw his brief as her lawyer. The Tata Group allowed Palkhivala to follow his conscience and to take this call. He spoke to the then law minister and famously told him: 'This is not negotiable. I am only informing you of my decision.'

He brought this same intellectual integrity to the corporate boardroom and even his famous budget speeches. As chairman of the Associated Cement Companies (ACC), he took difficult decisions that he firmly believed were in the interests of good corporate governance. In his annual budget speeches—if his analysis had revealed fundamental flaws in the budget document—he would not hesitate to be intensely critical of the finance minister of the day.

Because he was so candid, and also because he was such a powerful orator, Palkhivala's annual budget speeches were legendary and held the public spellbound. These speeches became so popular that they were eventually shifted, in 1983, to the Brabourne Stadium in Mumbai because no other venue in the city was large enough to accommodate the crowds. The famous cricketer Vijay Merchant once happily remarked: 'Mr Palkhivala has brought the crowds back to the Brabourne Stadium.' The context of this remark was that cricket Test matches, which always drew huge crowds in Mumbai, had moved away from the Brabourne Stadium a few years earlier to the nearby Wankhede Stadium. Mr Palkhivala's budget speeches, amazingly, had the same magnetic pull as Test cricket!

It is also because of these speeches that the second reason for his success comes to the fore. Despite being such a towering intellectual, he reflected humility and great respect for the people he interacted with. He was also very punctual. In fact, Farokh Subedar, my senior colleague who has served the Tata Group for several years, tells me how people could set their watch by Palkhivala's time of arrival for the budget address. He also recalls how Palkhivala would call young people to sit with him on the dais, behind the chairs or wherever space was available, if he noticed that the stadium was overflowing. At Bombay House, the headquarters of the Tata Group, Palkhivala would always accompany his visitors to the lift, and see them off with due courtesy, notwithstanding the pressures on his schedule.

This invaluable and rare combination of intellect and humility was accompanied by his extreme commitment to hard work. At the young age of twenty-nine, he worked intensely for twelve to fifteen hours each day, and this for several months at a stretch, to write his first book, *The Law and Practice of Income Tax*, co-authored with Jamshed Kanga. This book has served as a veritable Bible for students and practitioners of taxation in India.

His insatiable drive for hard work powered into his later life. He would painstakingly research material for his annual budget speech, including detailed meetings with heads of Tata Companies, to hear their views. Interestingly, no multitasking for him. He would focus on one task at a time, relentlessly— sometimes beginning a legal draft at 10.30 p.m. and completing it at 4.30 a.m. the next morning. His meetings were typically brief and to the point.

But perhaps the most important reason Nani Palkhivala led such a fulfilling life was his desire to contribute to the community and the nation. He was a trustee of the Sir Dorabji Tata Trust and the Sir Ratan Tata Trust, and played a key role in guiding their philanthropic activities. For many years, he was president of the Forum of Free Enterprise, which advocated a progressive, liberal economic agenda for the country. His biggest gift to the nation was undoubtedly motivated by this desire too—the victory he won in the Kesavananda Bharati case in the Supreme Court of India, where he argued continuously and relentlessly for five months, to protect the citizen's fundamental rights and the basic structure of the Indian Constitution.

The desire to serve the community guided many of his personal actions too. Dr S.S. Badrinath, founder of Sankara Nethralaya, Chennai, one of India's largest charitable eye hospitals, recounts the story of him being invited to dinner by Nani Palkhivala in Mumbai. After the meal, when Palkhivala was seeing the doctor to the car, he slipped him a small envelope, saying it was a token contribution for the hospital. When the doctor opened the envelope, he saw it contained Nani Palkhivala's personal cheque for Rs 2 crore. Later, when Palkhivala heard that they were going to place a plaque in the hospital to commemorate his name and contribution, he protested and requested that it not be done.

Palkhivala is a legend because he used his talents to the fullest, and for all the right purposes. He did so by living for what he believed in, by working very hard, respecting the people he worked with, and living his life with absolute grace and humility. These are the old-fashioned, timeless values that made this man a phenomenon. They are values that each of us can take to heart too, in our own lives, in whatever we do.

Our nation is proud of Nani Palkhivala and his legacy, for he continues to be an inspiration to us all.

22

The Ancient City of Pataliputra

Sir Ratan Tata, the younger son of Jamsetji Tata, founder of the Tata Group, lived more than a century ago. He played a remarkable role in excavating the ancient city of Pataliputra. The excavations that he championed and sponsored brought to life this great capital of the legendary Mauryan dynasty of India. Walk into history with me for a glimpse of this beautiful tale.

Patna is one of the most ancient cities of India. Its glories have been celebrated in arts and letters by poets and kings. As early as the 1780s, historians had tried to establish a connection between modern Patna and ancient Pataliputra. Were these two cities really the same? Indologists had suggested different sites for the modern location of the ancient city, and as early as 1895, some trial digs had also been conducted in the vicinity of Patna.

This was a dream project, not least because it held a piece of India's soul. The Mauryan dynasty, which ruled at Pataliputra, included the great emperor Ashoka, whose memory is sacred to our country. Indeed, the Ashoka Pillar, created by him, with its four lions and Ashoka Chakra, is today our official national emblem. Would these excavations unearth some more glories of Ashoka's kingdom?

Unfortunately, the site proved too large and complex, and the Archaeological Survey of India (ASI) was terribly underfunded and could not undertake such a task on its own. By 1903, the British Government of India was in no mood to sanction further expenses for deep digging. This is where Sir Ratan Tata stepped in.

Sir Ratan Tata was, by then, a wealthy man of commerce and industry. He was a connoisseur of art, an aesthete, a philanthropist and nationalist. He had donated liberally to the Non-cooperation Movement in South Africa led by Gandhi and had also extended financial support to Gopal Krishna Gokhale to set up the Servants of India Society. He was also keen on restoring and preserving his nation's rich heritage.

In 1912, Sir Ratan Tata indicated his keenness to support archaeological excavations in India and to rediscover for the country some of its precious history. After some initial discussions, Pataliputra was chosen as the site that he could support. He agreed to provide funds of Rs 20,000 a year—a large sum in those days—for an unlimited period of time. This would allow the ASI to undertake these excavations on a scale that it could simply not have imagined with its own resources.

The excavations were led by the archaeologist D.B. Spooner after various terms were agreed upon between Tata and the government in 1913. Interestingly, Spooner was the first American scholar to work in the Archaeological Department of British India. He had been trained at Stanford University, worked in Japan, and had also attended the Sanskrit College in Benares (Varanasi). Work began in right earnest at the carefully chosen site of Kumrahar in Patna with a large team. The ASI's report for 1913 says: 'The maximum number of labourers at any one time was something over thirteen hundred. It goes without saying that without Mr Tata's generosity, it would have been out of the question for the Department to have conducted the work on anything like this scale.'

For Spooner and his team, there was excitement, and some apprehension too. He could potentially unearth glories of one of the high points of Indian civilization, but he also had to deal with practical issues such as the high subsoil water level at the chosen site. At 10 feet below ground level, the team came across a series of old brick walls, but these were not as ancient as Pataliputra. So the digging continued, even deeper, in the search for Mauryan remains.

Finally, Spooner came across several fragments of pillars which bore evidence of Mauryan craftsmanship. He continued his efforts unabated. Then, on the morning of 7 February 1913, he was able to eventually piece together the plan of the grand ruins, with positions of several columns and pillars. This was a historic breakthrough. In his report, he happily concluded that 'the northern half of the Kumrahar site marked the position of a mighty pillared hall of Mauryan date, and thus the first structural building of the Mauryan period to be located in India . . .'

This was the start of the exciting discoveries at Patna, now established as the site of the ancient Pataliputra. Over the next four years, the excavation yielded significant quantities of coins, plaques and terracotta statuettes. The most important discovery was the location of Emperor Ashoka's 100-column throne room. Imagine for a moment, the legendary emperor and his court in council in this mighty, historic hall. This was the glory of ancient India coming to life all over again.

Sir Ratan Tata continued to support these excavations at Pataliputra, and his total contributions to the project amounted to Rs 75,000. He also took an active interest in their progress and continued to remain in touch with Spooner on a range of issues of historical interest. Unfortunately, in 1918, Sir Ratan Tata passed away at the relatively young age of forty-seven.

The antiquities excavated at Pataliputra were bequeathed to the nation and are now housed in the Patna Museum as the Sir Ratan Tata collection. At this museum, these beautiful finds continue to speak to us every day about the incredible heritage of this ancient city.

Sir Ratan Tata also owned a renowned collection of jade and European art, which he generously donated to the city of Mumbai. This beautiful collection is now exhibited at the Chhatrapati Shivaji Maharaj Vastu Sangrahalaya (Prince of Wales Museum), where it shines as a feast for the senses.

The voyage of restoring and nurturing India's art and heritage has been an ongoing journey for the Tata Trusts until today. Interestingly, in 2013, exactly a century after the Pataliputra excavations began, the Tata Trusts joined hands with the Aga Khan Foundation and the ASI to restore and rehabilitate Humayun's Tomb in Delhi. The exact shades of the five colours used in the original tomb—green, lapis blue, turquoise blue, yellow and white—were developed by conservation architects, alongside other techniques, to establish new standards in Indian conservation.

Our nation's rich cultural heritage is a part of its collective wealth. From the stately architecture of ancient cities and throne rooms to the bright colours of emperors' tombs to the vibrant art, craft and literature of our regions, we need to nurture and preserve our culture and history for our future generations. By visiting a nearby museum, or ensuring that our children read our epics, or learning much more about our beautiful native traditions, crafts and festivals, we can carry out our own small and interesting excavations too. There is a Pataliputra in each of our homes.

23

Tata and the Olympics

When an Indian wins a medal at the Olympics, we feel as if it is a personal victory; it fills us with pride. How can we forget P.V. Sindhu winning a silver medal at the 2016 Olympics at Rio, or shooter Abhinav Bindra winning gold at the Beijing Olympics in 2008, or, indeed, Mary Kom winning a boxing bronze medal at the London Olympics in 2012? When they stand on the victory podium, I think we stand there with them too.

The story of the Indian team's participation in the Olympics goes back to the year 1919, when Sir Dorabji Tata, the second chairman of the Tata Group, was chief guest at the Annual Sports Meet of the Deccan Gymkhana at Pune. He noticed that most of the athletes at the meet were peasants running barefoot, but were clocking creditable timings that were close to European standards.

Sir Dorabji, apart from managing the affairs of the Tata Group, was himself a keen athlete and excellent horseman, and he was also known to ride from Mumbai to Kirkee in nine hours flat. Even as he watched these peasant athletes in Pune, he was filled with a desire to see an Indian team participate in the Olympics. How could India, a proud nation, not field its own team at the largest and most prestigious sporting event in the world?

At his urging, Sir Lloyd George, the governor of Mumbai, took up the cudgels on behalf of Indian athletics and obtained affiliation for India with the international Olympic body.

Since an official Indian Olympics body did not exist at that time, Sir Dorabji decided to personally finance the first Indian team to the Antwerp Olympics in 1920. In fact, because there was no official body, a committee that he had helped establish selected the team as well.

In 1920, the first-ever Indian team to the Olympics marched proudly into the Antwerp Stadium. The team comprised four athletes and two wrestlers. P.F. Chaugule from Hubli and A. Dattar from Satara both ran the marathon and the 10,000 metre race. K. Kaikadi from Belgaum ran the cross-country race. G. Navale from Mumbai and N. Shinde from Kolhapur participated in the wrestling events. And Purma Banerjee from Bengal, who ran the 400 metre race, was the proud flagbearer who led the Indian team into the stadium. They came from very humble backgrounds, all these men, but they were selected for their natural talent based on previous performances.

As Dorabji Tata later wrote, in a personal letter addressed to the president of the International Olympics Committee, Count Baillet-Latour, in 1929:

> I therefore offered to arrange for the sending of three of the best runners to Antwerp to run the Olympic Marathon at the next meeting, when I hoped that with proper training and food under English trainers and coaches, they might do credit to India. This proposal fired the ambition of the nationalist element in the city, to try and send a complete Olympic team.

This first Indian team did not win any medals at the Olympics, but it planted the country's flag proudly and firmly at the Games. Thereafter, India has participated in every summer Olympics, without a single break.

Also, very importantly, Dorabji Tata returned from Antwerp with a conviction that the nation had to nurture a culture of sports that could give rise to many Olympians in the future. Using his personal resources, he sent Dr A. Noehren, physical director of the YMCA, out to visit every part of the country and evangelize sports and athletics. Four years later, Dorabji Tata once again bore some of the expenses to send the Indian team to the 1924 Paris Olympics. By now the Olympic spirit had caught on; the national team was funded significantly by various Indian states and consisted of seven competitors.

This pioneering sporting spirit eventually led to the formation of the Indian Olympic Association (IOA) in 1927, with Dorabji Tata as its first president, and Dr Noehren as secretary. The IOA selected India's team for the 1928 Amsterdam Olympics. This time around, the twenty-one-strong contingent also included a men's hockey team, championed by the Indian Hockey Federation.

Nine nations competed in hockey, and India was the only non-European team. The Indian team excelled in its preliminary games, beating Denmark, Belgium, Austria and Switzerland by wide margins. In the finals, in front of a large crowd of 23,400 people, India beat the Netherlands 3-0 to claim its first Olympic gold medal. The legendary Dhyan Chand was the top goal-scorer—he scored fourteen magical goals in that single tournament to stamp his name in gold.

Here was a dramatic and historic moment for our nation. The Indian hockey team had struck gold! This was the start of a string of Olympic gold medals for the Indian men's hockey team. Sir Dorabji Tata's dream to see India stand proud at the

Olympics had finally come true. He himself was selected as a member of the International Olympic Committee, yet another proud moment for India. A few years later, in 1932, Sir Dorabji passed away. India owes its first team participation in the Olympics and the creation of the Indian Olympic movement to him.

Since then, the Tata involvement with the Olympics and sports has come a long way. Over the years, the Tata Group itself has contributed an amazing number of Olympians to the country (more than fifty-two), including Baldev Singh, Levy Pinto, Charles Borromeo, Bahadur Singh, T.C. Yohannan, Deepika Kumari and Adille Sumariwalla. Each of their stories is inspiring, and they deserve separate chronicles altogether.

But I must end this story with yet another inspiring episode from the year 1947, just after India had won independence. This story is narrated in greater detail in the publication *Horizons*, conceptualized by Aman Nath for the Tata Group, and I have summarized it here.

Naval Tata (father of Ratan N. Tata), at that time a director of Tata Sons, was, like Sir Dorabji Tata, a sports enthusiast. He was also the president of the Indian Hockey Federation and very keen that the hockey team of newly independent India should participate in the 1948 Olympic Games in London. But it was difficult to raise funds, and time was rapidly running out. He happened to meet Lord Mountbatten in Mumbai, who suggested that Mr Tata raise this matter with Prime Minister Jawaharlal Nehru.

Naval Tata was given time at 10 p.m., late one night, to meet Nehru, who was extremely busy in the days post-Independence. The prime minister came into the meeting in a grumpy mood, feeling unhappy that he now had to talk about hockey, of all things, after a long day dealing with various pressing issues of national importance. He asked Tata: 'What if we didn't send our team to the meet?'

Naval Tata agreed that sending a team was not essential, but he also added: 'Would it not be an irony of fate that, at the very commencement of our national government, we do not send our team to defend our world title, won and retained for nearly twenty-five years during the colonial regime?'

Nehru's attitude transformed quickly. He instantly sanctioned Rs 1 lakh, a relatively large sum at that time, for the team's participation. He also facilitated a sports meet that could raise the rest of the funds required. The Indian hockey team was adequately funded and could go to London. And it won. In 1948, independent India won its first gold medal in hockey at the London Olympics. It went on to break all records by winning gold medals in the next two Olympics as well.

Let us reflect for a moment on India's first-ever Olympic team: Antwerp 1920, more than a century ago. It happened largely because Sir Dorabji Tata married his passion (for sports) to his life's purpose (nation-building). When we combine our passion and our purpose, even we can make magic happen.

24

Eka, the Indian Supercomputer

This is the story of Eka, the first Indian machine to feature among the ten fastest supercomputers in the world. Eka, a Tata product.

Way back in 1997, Deep Blue, a supercomputer created by IBM, defeated the world chess champion Garry Kasparov. It could evaluate an amazing 200 million positions on the chessboard in a single second. A few years later, Watson, again created by IBM, began winning tough game shows against humans.

These supercomputers captivated the imagination of mankind. They were incredibly fast and could solve complex problems with astonishing ease. They could help scientists in important areas such as weather forecasting, aerodynamic research, nuclear test simulation, car design and the development of life-saving drugs.

Hence, advanced countries such as the US, Europe, China and Japan all began investing in supercomputers. Unfortunately, until 2007, India did not have a powerful supercomputer on this list. For a country that wished to take its rightful place among the top economies of the world, this was an unpardonable omission.

S. Ramadorai, a Tata veteran who has been managing director and vice chairman of Tata Consultancy Services, the country's flagship IT services firm, was acutely aware of this gap. Discussing this subject, he once told me, 'The Tatas have had a history in this field. Way back in the 1980s, we had an association with Elxsi, who were working on large mainframe computers. We built some large machines, and TCS bought one of them. We used it primarily for research and development.' Other Indian organizations such as the Bhabha Atomic Research Centre (BARC) continued to actively pursue this area. However, PARAM, India's first supercomputer, created in 1991, never made it to the top echelons of this field.

Around 2000, TCS began recruiting scientists who were passionate about supercomputing and VLSI design. One such scientist was Dr Sunil Sherlekar, a prominent research scholar with a doctoral degree from IIT Bombay. Sherlekar was in contact with his classmate, Dr Narendra Karmarkar, the noted and highly cited Indian mathematician. Soon, their conversation turned to the area of supercomputing.

One day, Sherlekar made his way to Ramadorai's corner office.

'We would like to build a supercomputer,' he told Ramadorai. 'Will the Tatas support this?'

This was not merely an ambitious request; it was audacious in its intent, requiring significant technical and financial commitment. Yet, Ramadorai immediately saw the great impact such a project could have for the country and the Tata Group. He wrote out a note to Ratan Tata suggesting that this was an opportunity worth looking into.

Sherlekar recalls five meetings with Ratan Tata where the supercomputer proposal was discussed. Ratan Tata was excited but also insisted that a detailed business plan be chalked out to establish the economic rationale. Three different revenue streams were mapped out to generate the returns necessary to support such a large investment. This plan then became the blueprint for the project that envisaged the launch of a Tata supercomputer by November 2007. The machine, when ready, was to be the fastest in the world.

The board of Tata Sons, the holding company of the Tata Group, approved this plan in March 2006. It was a bold decision because for the country it was like going 'where no man had gone before'. A new company, Computational Research Laboratories (CRL), was established in Pune to implement the project. Intermediate milestones were defined and a team of brilliant research engineers began their work. There was excitement all around.

A prototype was first created, which was much smaller than the final version of the machine, but was an essential step in the journey. Then, in July 2007, there was an unexpected development that had the potential to derail the project. Karmarkar, one of the founder members, decided to quit the project because he had developed differences with the Tata Group on how the venture should progress.

A departure such as this could have paralysed the project, but the Tatas decided to persist. Ramadorai spoke to Sherlekar, who confirmed his and his team's confidence in taking the project forward. He saw no reason to give up the opportunity to create the country's first supercomputer that would feature among the world's fastest—a distinction that would live on in history forever. Sherlekar recalls an accidental meeting with Ratan Tata on the sidelines of a Tata Group conference during those anxious days.

'I was trying my best to avoid Ratan Tata, perhaps because my friend Karmarkar had left the project recently. Suddenly, I felt a tug at my elbow, and I turned around. It was Ratan Tata. He said: "You know, I am sorry we could not reach an agreement with Karmarkar. But you have a good team. I know you can take it forward." This was a wonderful gesture, and it touched me.'

The team took the project forward with determination. Ramadorai recalls: 'Finally, I decided that we had to proceed. We had to show the world that we had come of age in high-performance computing.'

Under Ramadorai's leadership, the machine was named 'Eka', which means 'one' in Sanskrit. The choice of a Sanskrit word illustrates the national pride inherent in this project. 'Eka' is all about the pioneering desire to be first, and symbolic of the many firsts that this supercomputer would eventually achieve.

The objective of the project was altered from a 1-petaflop machine to a 100-teraflop supercomputer with a lower investment, but it was to be ready by the original target date of 2007. It might not be the fastest in the world but it would have an excellent chance of making it to the top ten, a big breakthrough in itself for the country. To meet that year's deadline, the supercomputer had to be created latest by 31 October 2007.

Sherlekar and his team worked diligently round the clock. With less than seven weeks left to meet the October deadline, several technical challenges had to be mastered, including the challenges of cabling, cooling and interconnect technology. Each of these was addressed and its innovative solution was found. For instance, to ensure the required cooling, the Eka team developed a circular architecture for the machine.

Around 20 October, Eka was finally ready. But suddenly, a major problem reared its head. To be ranked among the top supercomputers, crossing a speed of 100 teraflops was essential. However, Eka was clocking only 97 teraflops in its pre-final tests again and again.

The Eka team remembered, from their experience, that there were some Russian scientists who could help with such a problem. The team found them somewhere in Mexico working with Intel. One of the young Eka engineers knew that Russian scientists generally loved Charminar cigarettes and Kingfisher beer. So he said to them: 'Help me solve this problem and I will send you an entire crate of Kingfisher beer!'

This generous offer of Indian beer appears to have helped immediately. The Russian scientists, after obtaining permission from their employer, helped the Eka team address the last pending problem. The matter was resolved just hours before the 31 October deadline. At 8.30 p.m. that evening, Eka went past the century mark and clocked 118 teraflops! At the end, there was a loud round of applause which appeared never-ending. And then there was a deep, respectful silence.

Eka immediately submitted its data to the committee that decides on the global supercomputer rankings. The team then had to wait until the rankings were announced. These were nail-biting moments. Would they achieve Ramadorai's target of being in the top ten in the world?

And then, on 6 November 2007, when the rankings were announced, Eka was fourth! The team had created the fourth fastest supercomputer in the world, beating machines from every other continent on their very first attempt.

Sherlekar was sleeping in his mother's home in Pune when he received a call well past midnight informing him of this wonderful news. He sent Ramadorai a text message on his mobile. He received an immediate response: 'Congratulations! India must announce this to the world.'

Soon, the world woke up to this news. The *Economic Times* said: 'The supercomputer named Eka, the first supercomputer to have been developed totally by a corporation without any government help, now shares the rarefied heights of supercomputing with two American and one German supercomputer.'

News of Eka's performance reached the corners of the supercomputing industry. There was collective global shock and surprise in finding out that India could achieve this coveted position, normally the domain of the richest countries of the world.

Eka was also put to good use very soon. The supercomputer was used in the launch of India's moon vehicle, Chandrayaan, by the Indian Space Research Organisation. One of the most challenging aspects here is predicting the weather at the time of the launch, and Eka did this perfectly. The then chairman of ISRO publicly expressed appreciation for the brilliant work done by Eka during this very successful launch.

Eka was also used in many other applications over the next few years—to develop new nanofluids, to improve the aerodynamics of cars, and, interestingly, to create India's first fully animated 3D feature film. However, for private enterprises, generating adequate commercial business on a continuing basis to make further investments behind such a supercomputer became a challenge.

No wonder that in the years thereafter, particularly given the large investments and the nature of applications involved, supercomputer development in our country has been taken forward primarily by the Government of India. Supercomputers that were much faster than Eka soon took birth. In 2020, the supercomputers Pratyush and Mihir, both developed by India's Ministry of Earth Sciences, rank among the top 100 in the world.

But way back in 2007, Eka put India firmly on the world supercomputing map. It was indeed 'one of its kind', and heralded a new era for India.

25

The Race

When J.R.D. Tata was just twenty-five years old, a news item in the *London Times* caught his attention. A unique air race had just been announced by His Highness the Aga Khan, spiritual leader of the Shia Imami Ismaili Muslims, to popularize aviation and flying in India. The announcement read:

> The Aga Khan has offered through the Royal Aero Club, a prize of UK Pounds 500, for the first flight from England to India, or vice-versa, by a person of Indian nationality. It must be a solo flight, completed within six weeks, from the date of starting. The prize will remain open for one year from 1st January 1930.

J.R.D. Tata was already an avid flyer, and he had just obtained his flying licence earlier that year. Since he was the first person to have qualified in India, his licence, issued by the Aero Club of India and Burma, proudly bore the number '1'. He was now inspired by the Aga Khan Prize and decided to take up the challenge that had been put forth. India to England, or the reverse direction, was an arduous route that involved several days of solitary flying over the sultry deserts, swamps and marshes of Iraq and the Iraqi city of Basra, and Egypt. Given the small biplanes of those years, the race to arrive first also involved several stopovers along the way.

Two other flyers had decided to take up the challenge, seized by the same excitement that gripped J.R.D. One of them was Manmohan Singh, an enthusiastic civil engineer with aeronautical training from Rawalpindi. The second was Aspy Merwan Engineer, a dashing young man who had obtained his flying licence at Karachi. So here was a race involving three people. The big question was who would win.

Manmohan Singh and Aspy Engineer decided to fly from England to India, whereas J.R.D. went the other way around—he began at Karachi and aimed to reach Croydon airport in England. Manmohan Singh's attempts were unfortunately not successful. He got lost in thick fog on a mountain road in southern Italy, and his aircraft, which he had intriguingly named 'Miss India', was severely damaged. He bravely persevered with the challenge, and made another fresh attempt after his aircraft had been set right. This time, he had to make a forced landing in a swamp near Marseille, and while he did eventually reach India, he could not make it in the stipulated time.

Meanwhile, Aspy Engineer had taken off from England in his second-hand de Havilland Gypsy Moth biplane on 25 April 1930. He was only seventeen years old. A superb aviator, he flew very well but encountered some engine trouble over Libya at Benghazi due to faulty spark plugs. But Aspy was well known for his mechanical and engineering skills, and so, despite these problems, he was able to safely land at the Aboukir airstrip near Alexandria in Egypt.

Here, Aspy parked his plane and immediately began his hunt for spark plugs in good condition, which would enable him to fly farther. But this was not easy in this far-flung location—it could take several days for these spark plugs to reach him. Valuable time would surely be lost.

We now turn our eyes to the third competitor in the flying race, J.R.D. Tata. Where was he? J.R.D. had taken off from Karachi on 3 May 1930 in a Gypsy Moth G-AAGI plane. He faced significant headwinds as he flew towards Jask, a small, hot and dusty town on the coast of Iran. There he stayed overnight and then took off towards Basra in Iraq. He drifted a little and had to double back from the salt marshes, north of Lingah, to reach Basra. From Basra, he flew towards Baghdad, and then towards Cairo.

En route, his faulty compass led him to drift out again and land in an old, disused World War I airstrip covered in anthills at Haifa. But he recovered quickly from this error and reached Cairo, where he was redirected to land at the Aboukir airstrip. In other words, he had reached the same airport near Alexandria where Aspy Engineer had parked his plane for some time now, searching for the elusive spark plugs which would enable him to resume his race.

What happened at Aboukir that day is beautifully chronicled by J.R.D. Tata's biographer, R.M. Lala. Here is what J.R.D. told Lala:

> At Alexandria, at 7 a.m., I saw another Moth parked there and realized it must be Aspy Engineer (my competitor) . . . When he heard that I had landed, he came out to the aerodrome to meet me. I asked him what he was doing there. He told me he was waiting for some spare plugs, since he had not taken an extra set of them. This was not very good planning! Since mine was a four-cylinder aeroplane, and I had eight spare plugs, I gave him four of them. He was so pleased and grateful that he insisted I take something from him, and he

gave me his Mae West life jacket. He had a Mae West, but no
spark plugs!

So the stranded Aspy Engineer got his spark plugs from his
competitor J.R.D., set his aircraft right, and took off towards
India. J.R.D. too got moving quickly but eventually lost further
time in Naples, where he landed late evening at a military
airfield. Here, because of strict army rules, he had to wait for
the military commandant to permit him to take off, for which
he lost four valuable hours. Thereafter, he flew uneventfully
towards Rome and Paris, and then the final leg from Paris to
Croydon in England.

However, by the time J.R.D. landed in Paris, Aspy Engineer
had already reached Karachi in India, and had won the Aga
Khan Prize. J.R.D. Tata had lost the flying competition by just
two hours and thirty minutes. The race was over.

But wait a moment . . . this is not the end of this story (as
we say in India, *kahaani abhi baaki hai, mere dost*). Twenty-
seven years later, in 1957, both men had grown significantly
in their careers and lives. J.R.D. Tata had become chairman of
the Tata Group and Aspy Engineer had joined the Indian Air
Force, where he had risen to become air vice marshal. A few
years later, Aspy would go on to become the second Indian to
head the Indian Air Force.

Aspy Engineer now wrote to J.R.D. Tata to greet him on
the twenty-fifth anniversary of India's first airline, which J.R.D.
had founded way back in 1932. J.R.D. was greatly moved by his
letter, and here is an extract from his reply to Aspy, dated 19
October 1957:

Of all the letters and messages I have received . . . none
pleased me more or brought back more pleasant memories
than yours . . . Those days were fun, weren't they? We were

both so much younger, particularly yourself . . . Although you were only seventeen or eighteen at the time, I at least did not underestimate you in the Aga Khan competition . . . I took you so seriously as a competitor that I spent at least a day more in checking everything on the plane and everything else connected with the trip.

J.R.D. goes on to say:

Our friendship ever since has been much more worthwhile than winning the competition would have been. I must say I enjoyed every moment of that adventure as I am sure you did too.

And then J.R.D. adds the concluding part of the story:

Incidentally, one of the highlights that remains imprinted on my memory was my arrival at Karachi by Imperial Airways, on my return to India (from England, after the race). When, to my embarrassment, you met me with a platoon of scouts and presented me with a medal. That was terribly nice of you, and so undeserved.

So, Aspy Engineer actually met his competitor J.R.D. on his return at Karachi airport and gave him a ceremonial welcome with a platoon, and a special medal too, for helping him win the race. What a graceful gesture, and one that must have surely brought a smile to J.R.D.'s face—and perhaps some tears too.

We all run and fly so many races in our lives. Winning some of them is important to us, but is this all that matters? And is it worthwhile to win them at any cost? Or is it far more important and meaningful, to help someone, to bring a smile to someone's face, whenever we can, along the way? And to nurture friendships that stand the test of time, which make our lives all the more fulfilling? As we search for our own answers, perhaps we can reflect on this beautiful old story of J.R.D. Tata and Aspy Engineer, both great men of our nation.

26

The Prime Minister's Relief Fund

On the eve of India's Independence, J.R.D. Tata sent out a very special message via telegram. It was timelined 7 p.m., 14 August 1947, and personally addressed to Jawaharlal Nehru, who was soon scheduled to take over as the first prime minister of free India. The telegram read:

DEAR JAWAHARLAL: ON THIS DAY MY THOUGHTS GO TO YOU WHOSE STEADFAST AND INSPIRED LEADERSHIP HAVE BROUGHT INDIA TO HER GOAL THROUGH THESE LONG YEARS OF STRUGGLE AND SUFFERING STOP I REJOICE THAT YOU WHO HAVE ALWAYS HELD SO HIGH THE TORCH OF FREEDOM ARE THE FIRST PRIME MINISTER OF FREE INDIA AND I SEND YOU MY HEARTFELT WISHES FOR SUCCESS IN THE HEAVY TASK OF GUIDING HER TO HER GREAT DESTINY STOP FROM JEH

Five hours later, at the stroke of midnight, India gained its freedom from British rule. Jawaharlal Nehru, addressing the nation, famously said:

> Long years ago, we made a tryst with destiny, and now the time comes when we shall redeem our pledge, not wholly or in full measure, but very substantially. At the stroke of the midnight hour, when the world sleeps, India will awake to life and freedom.

There was great rejoicing across the country. Two days later, Lord Mountbatten, the last British governor general of India, arrived at the Taj Mahal Hotel in Mumbai and addressed the audience from the stage of the ballroom in this famous hotel as part of the Independence Day celebrations. It was apt that his address was delivered at this historic property, built over forty years earlier by Jamsetji Tata as a proud symbol of India and Mumbai. Huge crowds gathered outside the hotel, shouting 'Jai Hind! Long live India! Love Live England!'

This was a most joyful time as India revelled in its freedom. But very soon, dark clouds appeared on this bright horizon. The partition of the country into India and Pakistan led to horrific riots and extensive loss of life and property. What began was perhaps the largest mass migration of people in human history as refugees streamed across the borders. It is estimated that as many as 20 million people were affected.

Responding to a call by the prime minister, the Tata Institute of Social Sciences (TISS) sent a special team of students to Delhi in October 1947 to help with the systematic registration of refugees, which would be very important to their resettlement in India. The team was sponsored by the Sir Dorabji Tata Trust and worked tirelessly to document the literacy, occupation, income and nature of employment and allocation desired by refugee families.

Their work was recognized by Jawaharlal Nehru himself. He said: 'We found the difference in their work and the work of many others who were earnest and had done their best, but who did not have the training to do it well. There is a difference between the trained workers and the merely enthusiastic workers.'

Notwithstanding such concerted efforts by multiple teams and by the government, it was becoming evident that the millions of refugees who had entered India from Pakistan would need significant support to alleviate their pain and loss. J.R.D. Tata was greatly concerned by this urgent national need and he was keen that the Tata Group should help as much as it could. He was also equally keen that the country should put in place a permanent, easily accessible platform for the raising of emergency funds to help in all such cases of distress. Perhaps the reports emanating from the TISS team further stoked his spirit of urgency in this regard.

Therefore, in October 1947, J.R.D. suggested to Pandit Nehru that a national fund for relief and distress should be created in the name of the prime minister himself to provide it with the required gravity and importance. He also stated that the Tatas would be happy to make a significant grant to such a fund.

J.R.D. Tata's biographer R.M. Lala has recorded that J.R.D. went on to tell the prime minister: 'If you have no such intention, could you advise me as to what we should do? In other words, I feel that such voluntary contributions should be used for meeting needs which cannot or would not be normally from government help.'

Clearly, J.R.D. felt strongly about the matter and pursued this national cause with vigour. It took a few weeks but the desired results were yielded. Two months later, on 11 December 1947, Prime Minister Nehru wrote back to J.R.D.:

My dear Jehangir,
There has been great delay in coming to some decision about the National Relief Fund. After consulting my colleagues here, we have arrived at some decisions which are incorporated in the attached note. I hope you approve of them.
Yours,
Jawaharlal Nehru

The note which Jawaharlal Nehru enclosed with his letter is an interesting piece of the nation's history. Here are some excerpts.

After consultation with various colleagues, it has been decided that a special fund should be opened, called the Prime Minister's National Relief Fund. This should be in the nature of a permanent fund to be utilized for any kind of relief of distress, but for the present, naturally, it should be applied for relief work for the refugees from the Panjab, the North West Frontier Province and other areas of Pakistan. Donors may earmark their donations for particular purposes.

The Trustees of the Fund should be: Prime Minister, Deputy Prime Minister, Finance Minister, President of the Indian National Congress, Chief Justice of India, A representative of the Tata trustees, a representative of Industry and Commerce, and possibly two other names of persons in their representative capacities. The treasurer of the fund should be the Auditor General of India.

Thus established, the Prime Minister's National Relief Fund rendered yeoman service to the nation over the next several decades. The Tatas had contributed to the fund immediately after it was set up in 1948, and it was established entirely with voluntary contributions from the public, including individuals, companies and trusts. In 1985, the management of the fund was entrusted entirely to the prime minister. The fund has rendered immediate relief to lakhs of families, including the relatives of those killed in natural calamities like floods, cyclones and earthquakes.

This, then, is the story of the genesis of the Prime Minister's National Relief Fund. An idea born in the mind of J.R.D. Tata and taken up by Prime Minister Nehru himself at J.R.D.'s urging. I often wonder how an industrialist like J.R.D., who must have been completely caught up in the pressures of managing his companies, particularly during the volatile period immediately post-Independence, always found the time and energy to relentlessly pursue these national causes wherever they struck him as being very important.

For instance, many years later, J.R.D. would bring the same energy and foresight when imploring the government to face the population problem of the country and the need for family planning. Perhaps the vision and purpose set out by the founder of the Tata Group, Jamsetji Tata, who felt the community and the nation should be centre stage in everything that the group does, was brightly and firmly in J.R.D.'s mind as he sat in the chair that was once occupied by Jamsetji himself.

There is no doubt that vision and purpose, once clearly defined, constitute the most important North Star in the life of any organization or individual. Whether it is J.R.D. Tata, you or me, our purpose motivates our actions even though finding our life's purpose is often a long and arduous search. Blessed are those who have found their purpose because their beacon then shines brightly.

27

Tata, Birla and the Bombay Plan

In January 1944, just three years before Indian Independence, a document was published that caused great consternation and concern amongst the British rulers of India. This pamphlet was priced at exactly Re 1 and immediately attracted a lot of attention. Indeed, it had to be reprinted a couple of times in India during the same year. And soon, Penguin published it in the United Kingdom. What was this document and why did it create all these ripples?

This was a comprehensive plan for the economic development of India, soon to be called the 'Bombay Plan', and it was authored by eight people. Because two of the authors were J.R.D. Tata and G.D. Birla, it would also be nicknamed in some circles the Tata–Birla Plan. It was a bold plan that called for massive investments in the industrial development of the country. In fact, it was the first-ever national economic plan for the Indian nation.

Lord Wavell, the then viceroy of India, was disturbed enough by this plan to write immediately to the Secretary of State in London. In his first letter, sent immediately after the plan had been published, he said: 'A considerable stir has been created by the Rs 10,000 crore economic plan for India.'

Thereafter, in May 1944, in a 'Private and Secret' letter, he added: 'I see the Bombay Plan has come out in the Penguin series. Sir Gregory, who takes criticism very much to heart, thought we should at once produce a rival pamphlet and broadcast it through the India office . . .'

Clearly, the British had been stung. Stung by the fact that Indians had moved far ahead of them in thought leadership for the future of India.

This thought leadership emanated from a stellar cast of eight Indian industrialists and technocrats who came together to build a plan for their beloved nation. Let's take a quick look at who they were.

There was J.R.D. Tata, who had taken charge as chairman of the Tata Group eight years earlier. G.D. Birla, head of the Birla Group of industries, ten years older than J.R.D., and already a well-respected senior leader. Lala Shri Ram, chairman of the DCM Group of Delhi, also a progressive Indian businessman. Kasturbhai Lalbhai, Ahmedabad-based industrialist and educationist. Purshottamdas Thakurdas, a Mumbai-based businessman, credited with building business associations.

Joining these five industrialists were three technocrats with fine minds, all from the Tata Group. Sir Ardeshir Dalal, A.D. Shroff and Dr John Mathai.

But why had this group of eight stalwarts decided to come together to build the Bombay Plan? As J.R.D. Tata has said, 'I knew Independence [for our country] was bound to come . . . I knew the country's economy would have to be tackled . . . that economic prosperity needed to reach not only the few but the many . . . businessmen and not only the Government should play a role.'

The committee initially engaged in broad deliberations on the economic future of the nation but later decided to articulate their views sharply and publicly as well through a published plan. J.R.D. Tata has credited this shift in approach to G.D. Birla. Here are J.R.D.'s words of praise for Birla (extracted from J.R.D. Tata's biography by R.M. Lala):

> G.D. Birla was a man of high intelligence and knowledge. When we were floundering to find a structure in the first few meetings, it was he who suggested—It is difficult to forecast what India should do after being free . . . so let's do it this way—first estimate to get the people the kind of standard of living they want. What is needed? So many calories of food requiring so many tons of grain, so many metres of cloth, housing, schools, etc.

This quantitative approach to planning could be seen throughout the pages of the Bombay Plan. For instance, the plan pointed out that a large proportion of Indians were not getting enough food to eat despite the fact that India was an agricultural country. It then built a plan for food supplies which took into account a well-balanced nutritive diet of 2600 calories per adult person per day—and actually went on to detail the weight of cereals (16 ounces), pulses (3 ounces), vegetables (6 ounces), fruits (2 ounces), milk (8 ounces) that would hence be needed for this purpose. And finally, it calculated that an annual expenditure of Rs 2100 crore would be required to deliver this nourishment to India's population of 389 million people at the time.

Having set out a total requirement of Rs 10,000 crore for food, clothing, housing, education and industry, the Bombay Plan then outlined the various sources of funds which could be used. Interestingly, the first source of funds it highlighted was the hoarded wealth of the country, mainly gold.

In addition, it called for funding from sterling securities held by the Reserve Bank of India, favourable balance of trade, foreign borrowings, national savings, heavier taxation of unearned income, and, finally, new money to be printed by the government.

Very importantly, the Bombay Plan put forward a framework for rapid development of basic industries such as power, mining, engineering, armaments and transport; as well as consumer industries such as textiles, glass, leather and oil. This was the first systematic approach to the economic development of free India.

Overall, it was a bold, imaginative and radical plan with a fifteen-year timespan. It was a daring attempt because the underlying assumption was that as soon as World War II concluded, the British would hand over power to a popular government, which would have the economic freedom to implement this plan, independent of any colonial ruler. In other words, these Indian industrialists were, in effect, telling the British to hand over power to Indians and quit the country.

No wonder the plan made the British jittery and uncomfortable. But, in addition, it also created a storm amongst various segments of Indians. Gandhians thought the plan was against Gandhi's ideology. Conservative Indian businessmen considered it too far-fetched. Leftists found it reactionary and a half-hearted compromise, and soon published their own plan in response.

J.R.D. Tata was unfazed by all these reactions. Addressing the Rotary Club of Bombay on 15 February 1944, he launched a bold defence of the plan to underscore why it was needed. Concluding his speech, he said, 'That there should be widespread poverty and misery, in a country so naturally endowed by providence with manpower, talent and natural resources, is an intolerable paradox, and a disgrace which should fill us with shame and anger, and a burning desire to wipe out this terrible wrong done to our people. The obstacles, doubts and setback which may have to be faced [in taking forward this plan] should not deflect us from our task, but rather arouse us to greater endeavour.'

In many ways, the Bombay Plan, pioneering in its intent and incredibly broad in its sweep, provoked the political leadership and also conditioned the nation to the post-Independence economic plans which were to follow. Unfortunately, there is no evidence that Jawaharlal Nehru, the first prime minister of India, ever regarded the Bombay Plan seriously enough. But what was exemplary and unique was the coming together of so many industrialists, perhaps fierce rivals in the marketplace, to converge and create an economic plan for the country. I wish I could have attended some of these meetings to see these legendary minds work together.

Many years later, in 1986, R. Venkataraman, the then vice president of India (he would go on to become president), recalled the Bombay Plan as one of J.R.D. Tata's key contributions to India. J.R.D., then eighty-two years of age, responded quite simply: 'My only contribution to it was to arrange for the Bombay Plan to be written. It [the drafting of the plan] was done mainly by Dr John Mathai, but after considerable discussion.'

Those graceful words do not take away from the fact that the Bombay Plan is the first-ever instance, anywhere in the world, of leaders of industry stepping out of their boundaries, and collaborating amongst themselves, to prepare a national economic plan. And then, they also did their best to educate people that systematic planning was essential for rapid economic development.

Were they merely leaders of industry, these great men, or were they much more?

28

A Mission of Learning

In January 1944, five Indian industrialists, including J.R.D. Tata and G.D. Birla, and three Tata technocrats, published the Bombay Plan—the first-ever plan for the long-term economic development of post-Independence India. The plan had stung the British because it proved that Indians were capable of planning their own future.

Now, these industrial leaders were eagerly looking forward to Indian freedom, and to actively contributing to the economic development of the country post the end of World War II. In fact, Indian industry had also contributed handsomely towards the Allied War efforts over the past several years. Now the Allies, including the British, were on the verge of defeating the Axis, led by Adolf Hitler.

Perhaps in recognition of this contribution, the British Government of India announced, in October 1944, an industrial mission to the US and UK. The mission was to take place sometime in 1945 and would comprise some of India's most famous industrialists, who would bear their respective expenses throughout the trip. The objective was to study how the industry had successfully organized itself as well as technical advancements in these two developed nations. The government announcement added: 'The knowledge and ideas which they [the Indian industrialists] will bring back with them will be of great value in the further industrialization of the country, after the war.'

Many authors of the Bombay Plan including J.R.D. Tata, G.D. Birla and Kasturbhai Lalbhai were invited on this mission to the West, as were several other famous Indian businessmen. Coordinating on behalf of the Government of India was H.M. Patel, ICS, the then secretary of industry and civil supplies (he would later become finance minister of India in the Janata government regime). Detailed arrangements with various overseas companies and factories were put in place over several months of planning, and the delegation was eventually all set to leave India in the second week of May 1945.

However, just a few days before they embarked on their flight, an unanticipated development occurred. Mahatma Gandhi issued a strong statement opposing the industrial mission. On 6 May 1945, he contacted the press from Mahabaleshwar. This statement was reported by the *Bombay Chronicle* the very next day under the sensational headline 'Gandhiji's Bombshell for Industrialists':

> Ask them to wait till leaders are free. Freedom will come only after big business forego crumbs from Indo-British loot . . . All the big interests proclaim with one voice that India wants nothing less than her own elected National Government to shape her own destiny free of all control, British or other. This independence will not come for the asking . . . The so-called unofficial deputation which will go to England and America dare not proceed, whether for inspection of for entering into a shameful deal, so long as the moving spirits of the Congress

Working Committee are being detained without any trial for
the sole crime of sincerely striving for India's Independence
without shedding a drop of blood, save their own.

Clearly, the Mahatma was totally and rightly preoccupied with
thoughts of his colleagues fighting for freedom who had been
unjustly imprisoned by the British. It is also not clear from
historical evidence whether Gandhiji had with him all the facts
about the delegation before issuing his statement, in particular
the fact that this was only a learning mission and not meant
for signing any business deals with the UK or US. On the other
hand, for the industrialists, the future economic development
of their country was an equal priority and this mission was a
stepping stone towards that goal.

J.R.D. and G.D. Birla were shocked by Gandhiji's statement.
G.D. Birla, who knew Gandhiji very well, sent him a telegram
on 7 May: 'I am very much pained and I refuse to believe that
you could have given a public expression of distrust in the
bonafides of myself, Tata and Kasturbhai, whom you have so
well known . . . your statement sure to be construed as strong
denunciation of our motives whereas you usually refrain from
expressing any opinion when you do not know full facts . . .'

On 8 May 1945, J.R.D. Tata issued a communiqué to
the press, clarifying the purpose of the delegation, which, he
highlighted, was in fact patriotic, and 'to gain such knowledge
and experience which would enable us to play a better part in
India's economic development'. He also clarified that there
would be no 'shameful deals'. He went on to say that India
could not afford to stand still (on the economic front) while
other nations, great and small, were forging ahead.

Then, on 9 May, J.R.D. Tata also wrote to Gandhiji,
expressing himself candidly through a personal letter.

My dear Gandhiji,

You must have seen my statement to the press on the communiqué you issued a couple of days ago, on the subject of our forthcoming visit to England and America.

I cannot tell you how hurt I was by the views you expressed about our trip, and the strong language you used.

What made it worse was that I, or some other member of the Group, was not given an opportunity of removing the misapprehensions which you evidently entertained about the purpose of our trip. In the circumstances, I was driven to issue my statement to the press, in order to make my position clear.

I am leaving on Friday morning and expect to return some time in August, when I hope I shall have an opportunity of discussing the matter with you.

With kind regards and sincere wishes,

Yours sincerely,
J.R.D. Tata

Gandhiji must have read these candid messages and reflected on them deeply. He may have come to the considered conclusion that this industrial mission to the West was indeed in the country's interests because it would enable these industrialists to bring best practices back to India and prepare their industrial houses for post-Independence development.

It is a great tribute to the Mahatma that he then decided to respond quickly and personally, both to G.D. Birla and J.R.D. Tata, indicating to them in his own nuanced manner that he was comfortable with the purpose of the delegation. To J.R.D. Tata, he sent a handwritten note from Mahabaleshwar, dated 20 May 1945:

Bhai Jehangirji [this is in the Gujarati script, rest of the letter in English],

I have your angry note, if you can ever write anything angry.

If you have all gone not to commit yourselves to anything, my note protects you. My answer is to the hypothetical question. If the hypothesis is wrong, naturally the answer is wrong, and is therefore protective of you all. There was no question of my referring to any of you, as I was dealing with an assumption. I hope I am clear.

M.K. Gandhi

This is such a brilliantly crafted piece of communication given the context. Gandhiji was a master communicator, whether it was to the people of India at large or the country's leading industrialists. His reassuring note set matters to rest immediately.

The industrial mission, which included J.R.D. Tata and G.D. Birla, took place and was a great success. The delegates visited factories in England and America, keeping to strenuous day-long schedules for several weeks, and learnt about modern machinery. On their return to India, they issued a detailed report, which concluded as follows: 'We have returned from our trip enriched with first-hand knowledge . . . and better informed appreciation of the significance, scope, needs and complexities of modern industry.'

The delegation also underlined their realization of the importance of massive scientific research and education for the progress of the nation. I think this realization may well have contributed to J.R.D. Tata redoubling his focus on TIFR, which had opened its doors earlier that year, and which went on to become the cradle of atomic energy research in India. Perhaps it was also one key factor that influenced G.D. Birla in his decision to establish a modern engineering college, which later became BITS, Pilani—one of the country's finest.

Thus, the creation of the Bombay Plan in 1944, followed by the industrial mission to the West in 1945, played a key role in sharpening the thoughts of major Indian industrialists about what lay ahead and how best they could contribute to national economic progress. They were patriots at heart, and as industrialists, they also knew that they had to play a key role in the rapid economic growth of their beloved nation—essential to lift India from the poverty and distress caused by colonial rule. Therefore, they also made the additional effort to immediately address the occasional misunderstanding that is inevitably part of any political–economic landscape, particularly during emotionally charged times.

Indeed, an invaluable mission of learning.

29

Toilet Rolls and a Speech

J.R.D. Tata, who served as chairman of the Tata Group for over five decades, was a stickler for excellence and perfection. Here are three simple and memorable stories which can inspire us to excellence in our own lives.

J.R.D. Tata would often fly Air India, the airline that he had founded in the 1930s. Meher Heroyce Moos, who joined Air India as an air hostess way back in 1965, has written a warm tribute about how J.R.D. would 'walk the length of the aircraft, checking out the galleys, the equipment used, the furnishings, whether the curtain had frayed, or whether dust was found on the lower edges, the crew's interaction with the passengers and above all the quality of the meal services'.

Once, on an Air India flight, J.R.D. was travelling with L.K. Jha, one of the senior-most bureaucrats in the Indian government. Suddenly, J.R.D. went missing from his seat for a long time, nearly an hour. L.K. Jha was naturally concerned, and, when J.R.D. returned, he asked him where he had gone.

J.R.D. replied that he had wanted to see if the toilets on the aircraft were clean and all arrangements were as per specifications. But Jha was still not convinced because just a mere inspection of a few toilets would not take an hour. So he persisted with his query. J.R.D. eventually responded: 'The toilet rolls had not been placed properly.'

Jha was amazed at what had actually transpired. J.R.D. Tata, chairman of the airline, had gone to each toilet on the aircraft to ensure that the toilet rolls had been placed as they should have been. He had then personally corrected any wrong placements. This singular attention to the smallest detail undoubtedly had its impact on every member of the team and made Air India one of the finest airlines in the world.

Yet another vignette is narrated by Jitender Bhargava, who had joined Air India in 1989 as head of public relations. On 15 October 1992, he was waiting at the Oberoi Hotel to receive J.R.D. Tata for a party to celebrate the diamond jubilee of Air India. The party was due to start at 9.30 p.m., and as Bhargava began escorting J.R.D. from the entrance of the hotel to the poolside, which was the venue of the event, J.R.D. told him: 'Sorry young man, I am late.'

Bhargava expectedly said, 'No, sir.'

J.R.D. Tata immediately pulled up his coat sleeve and showed Bhargava his wristwatch. It showed 9.33 p.m., a delay of three minutes. The delay may have been small, but J.R.D. nonetheless felt the need to apologize for not being perfectly on time.

The third story is narrated superbly by J.R.D. Tata's biographer, R.M. Lala. Once, a young economist working with the Tata Group, D.R. Pendse, was invited to speak at an international conference in London in 1979. J.R.D. Tata heard of this invitation, called Pendse to his office, and asked for the text of his speech.

Pendse responded to J.R.D. that he normally spoke extempore. J.R.D. exclaimed, 'You mean you will address an international audience of 500 people without an address in your pocket. Have you rehearsed your speech?'

Pendse admitted that he had not rehearsed his speech either, but was proposing to do it in the London hotel the day before the event. J.R.D. was not happy with this proposal, and immediately told him, 'Your audience will hear you, but have you heard yourself? Keep a tape recorder in front of you every time you rehearse at home and play it back. Then you will know how the audience is going to hear you.'

J.R.D. also advised the young Pendse that although he may know the topic of the speech—economics—very well, he should nonetheless prepare rigorously and talk slowly. Then, because Pendse did not own a tape recorder, J.R.D. picked up his own and lent it to him. 'Take this. Write your speech. Rehearse at home. Listen. Then you can return it to me. I will find another recorder for the meantime. Don't worry, and good luck to you.'

Pendse promptly changed tack, as advised by his chairman, and practised his speech. He then delivered a brilliant address at the London conference, which was met with a standing ovation. Pendse tells R.M. Lala: 'It was beyond my expectations. And as I sat down acknowledging it [the applause], I could almost feel the chairman smiling at me.'

D.R. Pendse later went on to become the economic adviser to the Tata Group. What was remarkable is that J.R.D. Tata, chairman of a large industrial group, found the time and energy to speak to his young economist and advise him on the rigour and discipline required regarding excellent preparation for a speech.

J.R.D. followed this practice in his own life too. He wrote his own speeches, often correcting them several times in his handwriting until they met his high standards of excellence. It was not unusual for his speeches to have four or five interim drafts, and he would often refuse an invitation to speak unless he had adequate time to prepare very well.

All these stories are rooted in one of the key guiding principles of J.R.D. Tata's life. In his own words: '. . . one must forever strive for excellence, or even perfection, in any task however small, and never be satisfied with the second best.'

Do we follow this simple but powerful principle in our own lives? Success would be a natural outcome when we pursue such excellence, and we would also feel far more fulfilled in every endeavour that we undertake.

30

Lady Meherbai Tata: Feminist Icon

Lady Meherbai Tata was born in 1879, and went on to become a feisty pioneer in the cause of women's rights in India. A versatile, intelligent and accomplished lady, she was also a keen sportsperson and an accomplished pianist.

She was consulted on the milestone act which made child marriage illegal in India. It was called the Sarda Act, and was passed in 1929. Lady Tata evangelized this progressive and radical move in all quarters, both in India and overseas, and also spoke against untouchability and the purdah system. She was deeply committed to the cause of women's education in India, and was one of the founders of the National Council of Women.

On 29 November 1927, she spoke in favour of the Hindu Marriage Act at Battle Creek College (now Andrews University) in Michigan, USA. Her spirited speech there provided her audience an excellent overview of Indian culture and history, as well as the customs and ignorance which impeded the progress of women in the country. She then called upon the Government of India to expeditiously pass a proposed bill which would outlaw child marriage and thus end this social evil. Indeed, she was a powerful spokesperson for the women of India. Along with her husband, Sir Dorabji Tata, the second chairman of the Tata Group, she also met the then US president, Calvin Coolidge, at the White House.

Despite being married into a wealthy family, she kept in active touch with all segments of society. One particular story is very interesting. When she heard that women living in a poor area of Byculla in Mumbai were unable to get access to food because of riots, she offered to become a food and vegetable vendor herself, along with some of her lady colleagues. The mayor refused her request, saying that his team and he did not consider it graceful for distinguished ladies to sell food. To which Lady Tata responded with quiet dignity: 'We ladies did not come here to be graceful, we came here to be useful.'

She was fiercely independent in her thoughts and actions. One powerful testament to this is her name: Meherbai. Her father, H.J. Bhabha, who was a professor and an eminent educationist based in Bangalore and then Mysore, played a key role in introducing her to progressive Western ideas. But when he wished to also change her name in a Western fashion, she drew the line firmly. When she was studying in school in Bangalore, he wanted her to spell her name in its anglicized version, 'Mary'. She resisted this, stood up to her father and insisted on retaining her name in its original Persian form, 'Mehri', which thereafter became Meherbai. This demonstrated her pride in her roots and culture.

This deep pride expressed itself in other ways too. Meherbai was fond of playing tennis, and became very proficient at this sport. In fact, she won over sixty prizes in tennis tournaments. She was the first Indian woman drawn to play Olympic tennis—the mixed doubles in the Paris Olympics of 1924. What is most interesting and unique is that she played all her tennis matches wearing the Parsee saree, driven by her pride in her nation, and perhaps also to make a point to the British, who were ruling India at that time.

Her husband and she would often be sighted at the Centre Court of Wimbledon, watching tennis matches there. Meherbai's passion for sports went beyond tennis too—she was an expert horse rider, and among the first Indian women to fly, as a passenger in the Zeppelin airship, in 1912.

One of the most memorable stories I have heard about this inspiring woman is about the beautiful diamond she owned—and later gave away. The Jubilee diamond, at 245 carats, was twice as large as the famous Kohinoor, and bought for her by her loving husband. Lady Meherbai Tata wore it to special events on a fine platinum chain. However, in the 1920s, Tata Steel (then called TISCO) went through a great financial crisis and was on the verge of collapse. To resolve this crisis, the Jubilee diamond, which was part of their personal wealth, was pledged to Imperial Bank by Dorabji Tata and Meherbai to raise funds. This did solve the problem, and Tata Steel lived on to prosper greatly. Later, this diamond was sold, and the proceeds were used for the creation of the Sir Dorabji Tata Trust, which has been at the forefront of so many philanthropic activities in India. Earlier in this book, this fascinating story is narrated in far greater detail.

Lady Meherbai Tata played an enthusiastic role in raising contributions during World War I, and was an active member of the Indian Red Cross Society at that time. In 1919, in recognition of her services to women's progress, and to the war efforts, she was made a Commander of the British Empire and received this honour at the hands of King George V.

Lady Meherbai Tata died of leukaemia in 1931, after a courageous fight against this terrible disease. Sir Dorabji Tata founded a Trust in her memory, which was dedicated to cancer research. This mission against cancer eventually led to the founding of the Tata Memorial Hospital in Mumbai in 1941.

Her ashes were interred at a cemetery at Brookwood in England, on a plot of land adjacent to the resting place of the founder of the Tata Group, and her father-in-law, Jamsetji Tata. Later, this would also be the final resting place of her beloved husband, Sir Dorabji Tata.

The words on her tombstone read: 'She died as she had lived, working nobly for the cause of the women and the country, which she loved and served so well.'

May her life continue to inspire all of us.

31

Dr John Matthai: A Man of Many Parts

Dr John Matthai was a fascinating man. A powerful intellectual with an equally powerful voice, he was a director of the Tata Group for many years. He was a close associate of J.R.D. Tata, and one of the principal authors of the Bombay Plan, which created a storm in India in the 1940s.

Dr Matthai was a distinguished student who began his life as a lawyer and went on to earn his doctorate in economics. He was the first Indian to obtain a DSc in economics at the London School of Economics. He then served as a professor in Madras University, teaching economics at Presidency College. This was followed by a stint as director general of commercial intelligence and statistics.

He joined the Tata Group in 1940, only two years after J.R.D. Tata had taken charge as chairman. He served as adviser to J.R.D., and also as director-in-charge of Tata Chemicals for two years. In 1944, he helped author an extraordinary document called the Bombay Plan.

This pioneering plan for the economic development of India evolved under the guidance of leading Indian industrialists, including J.R.D. Tata, G.D. Birla and Kasturbhai Lalbhai—well before the government's own five-year economic plan was conceived. It called for massive investments in roads, railways and power—which are essential for the country's progress even today. On account of its radical proposals, the plan caused great discomfiture to nearly everyone—British rulers, leftists, Gandhians and many businessmen. In essence, the Bombay Plan reflected a view that industry should play a key role in national development, a theme which has always been central to the Tata Group. Elsewhere in this book, you will find a story that narrates many more details of the Bombay Plan. Speaking many years later in 1986 about the writing of this plan, J.R.D. Tata said, 'It was done mainly by Dr John Matthai, but after considerable discussion.'

In 1946, Dr Matthai was invited to join Pandit Jawaharlal Nehru's cabinet in the Interim Government of India—a tribute to his intellectual capabilities. He joined as minister for railways and transport, then held the commerce and industry portfolio, and was eventually elevated to serve as minister for finance. But shortly thereafter, he developed differences with Prime Minister Nehru, because he felt that India was not ready for a Planning Commission and centralized planning in those early days. Therefore, he resigned from the government as a matter of principle, and returned to the Tata Group in 1950.

In his second stint with the Tatas, Dr Matthai served as director-in-charge of Tata Steel (then called TISCO) and Tata Motors (then called TELCO). He was also chairman of the Sir Dorabji Tata Trust. In this role, he helped establish the Demographic Research Institute in 1956, which is today the International Institute for Population Studies. He also played a key part in setting up the Tata Agricultural and Rural Training Centre for the Blind.

Dr Matthai was known for having a dignified demeanour in everything that he said and did. His colleague in the Tata Group, Sir Homi Mody, once said of him, 'He has got many natural advantages: face, figure, manner, voice, all that and invested with an air of profundity in everything he said. Even if Dr Matthai said "Good morning", it sounded like a papal benediction.'

He was a versatile professional, becoming chairman of the newly constituted State Bank of India, and serving as vice chancellor of two universities: Bombay University, between 1955 and 1957, and, thereafter, Kerala University, in his home state. Always close to his roots as an economist, he was also the first president of the National Council of Applied Economic Research (NCAER).

An avid reader, he was also the first chairman of the National Book Trust of India. 'Good books,' he once said, 'deserve to be read many times over and can be a continuing source of pleasure.' He continued to read actively into his ripe old years post retirement, saying that he was occupying himself with 'a certain amount of desultory reading'.

J.R.D. Tata relied greatly on Dr Matthai's advice on many subjects of importance, and particularly in sensitive areas which required deep judgement and wisdom. After Dr Matthai retired from the Tata Group in 1957 and left Mumbai to settle down in Kerala, J.R.D. reflected this in a personal letter: 'Throughout the years we have been together, you have been a wonderful source of strength and comfort to me. I always felt that I could turn to you when troubled or uncertain about any matter, and get from you advice which would never compromise on fundamentals, particularly where the prestige of the firm and the country was involved.'

Dr Matthai called his years in the Tata Group the best part of his life. 'The work was very interesting,' he said, and added, 'they maintain a very high standard of business. I was never called upon to compromise on any matters; nor once was I asked to do anything which I could not justify to my conscience.'

Dr Matthai was awarded the Padma Vibhushan, the country's second highest civilian honour. He passed away in February 1959 at the age of seventy-three after living a life that was so rich and which contributed significantly to the nation. I often think how wonderful it would have been to personally know and interact with this towering and versatile intellectual who gave so much of his life to the Tata Group and to the country he loved.

32

A Temple for the Performing Arts

Zubin Mehta has made our nation proud many times over. He is one of the most talented and best-known conductors of Western classical music on our planet and has received honours from around the world. In April 2016, the music maestro celebrated his eightieth birthday with two stirring concerts at the National Centre for the Performing Arts (NCPA) in Mumbai. Back in his beloved home town, he led the Israel Philharmonic Orchestra in front of a spellbound audience.

The music was phenomenal, and it enthralled everyone. Every note and every movement fed the soul. What added to the magic were the brilliant acoustics—the music swept around you, clear and distinct, with not a touch of background noise. And, of course, there could not have been a more magnificent venue than the Jamshed Bhabha Theatre at the NCPA with its technical excellence, historic 100-year-old marble staircase, and dazzling foyer.

No wonder legends like Zubin Mehta perform at the NCPA, among the finest venues for the performing arts in our country. Other notable artists who have performed at this venue include M.S. Subbulakshmi, Ustad Vilayat Khan, Birju Maharaj, Kelucharan Mohapatra, Parveen Sultana and Yehudi Menuhin. In 2017, at this same venue, the playwright Girish Karnad received the Tata Literature Live! Lifetime Achievement Award, and delivered a graceful acceptance speech even while carrying his breathing apparatus by his side. Today, the NCPA receives great acclaim but its story began in a dream, dreamt over fifty years ago, by Jamshed Bhabha, a senior director of the Tata Group. Here is the story of that dream.

Jamshed Bhabha was the younger brother of Homi Bhabha, the father of India's atomic energy programme. He was also a trustee of the Sir Dorabji Tata Trust, established in the name of the second chairman of the Tata Group. In 1966, Bhabha first proposed a cultural complex that could preserve the rich legacy of India's traditions in dance, music and drama. It would have grand performance spaces and would also be research-oriented, archiving the country's heritage. In scale and vision, it would be similar to the Kennedy Center in Washington DC or the Lincoln Center in New York.

J.R.D. Tata saw the merit of this idea and supported it. But the proposal soon met with a lot of scepticism. Some people questioned the need to spend a lot of money on building such a grand cultural complex in a relatively poor country like India. Others simply questioned the space it would require and the idea of shelling out significant funds.

Like with any visionary idea, building the NCPA involved challenges that initially looked unsurmountable. But these were not to stop J.R.D. and Jamshed Bhabha. They were charged with the power of the dream. J.R.D. Tata, defending this dream, famously said, 'While we want to build a prosperous society, we do not want it to be merely a materialistic, consumer society. Apart from the fact that a nation like ours, with its ancient civilization, cannot afford to neglect the cultural heritage handed down to it over the centuries.'

The issue of the land went through several discussions too, including an initial offer of land near the Ellora caves. But that was too far away. Eventually, the government agreed to let the Sir Dorabji Tata Trust reclaim land from the sea at Nariman Point at the tip of south Mumbai and build the centre on this reclaimed land that would then be leased out to the Trust. An arduous task. Then there was also the matter of funds.

To support the project, the Sir Dorabji Tata Trust immediately agreed to provide a grant of Rs 40 lakh, a large sum in the 1960s, which primarily covered the costs of land reclamation. The project began quickly thereafter. Archival photographs of that time show land being reclaimed out of the waters and the foundation stone being laid, once again in the presence of J.R.D. Tata and Jamshed Bhabha. These leaders also took a conscious decision not to feature 'Tata' in the name of this centre for it was dedicated to the nation.

On 29 December 1969, the NCPA was inaugurated by Prime Minister Indira Gandhi, albeit in temporary premises provided by the Bhulabhai Desai Memorial Trust. She quoted a Sufi proverb in her inaugural address: 'If I had two loaves of bread, I would sell one and buy hyacinths to feed my soul.' That was indeed the essence of Jamshed Bhabha's dream—music, dance and theatre to feed the nation's soul and nurture its heritage.

Meanwhile, on 8 acres of reclaimed land, the magnificent structure of the permanent NCPA complex, designed by the architect Philip Johnson, was starting to take shape. Many other charitable trusts and corporates also came forward with financial support. The centre was eventually completed in 1980. The inaugural concert at the Tata Theatre was a shehnai recital by the legendary musician Ustad Bismillah Khan. How beautiful and ethereal that evening must have been, I wonder, in the hands of a master musician who revelled in the sounds of his beloved woodwind instrument.

In the years since, as India's premier institution of the performing arts, the NCPA has been the proud host to several thousand programmes across all major performing art forms. It offers multiple venues within a single campus—the Tata Theatre, Jamshed Bhabha Theatre, Experimental Theatre, Godrej Dance Theatre and Little Theatre. It is a lush, calm oasis of art in the country's commercial capital.

The NCPA has also undertaken special projects to record the musical heritage of India, all the way from small villages and towns, and has even used an acoustically treated van to record the voices of local artists. These recordings are now part of its fabulous music library. The impressive Symphony Orchestra of India, based in the NCPA, is India's first and only professional orchestra.

Jamshed Bhabha continued to champion the cause of the NCPA throughout his lifetime, till his death in the year 2007. Amazingly, this visionary of the arts also willed everything he had to the NCPA—from modern paintings and silver artefacts to his large sea-facing bungalow on Malabar Hill called the Mehrangir, which was auctioned only a few years ago for the handsome sum of Rs 372 crore. This significant amount of money has helped fortify an institution that attempts to constantly put the performing arts centre stage, no matter what the circumstances.

The NCPA is managed by an independent trust today, headed by the very committed and capable Khushroo Suntook, a Tata veteran himself. He is determined that the NCPA should live up to the vision of Jamshed Bhabha, its founder, who gave so much of himself to create this national centre. And that is so true because for Jamshed Bhabha, this magnificent institution was a labour of love. He persisted through all the early struggles, he made the NCPA happen, and he committed a large part of his life to it—because he believed that preservation of our culture is essential to our national fabric.

When something we strongly believe in becomes a labour of love for us, life takes on a new meaning and our dreams tend to come alive.

33

Who Was Nevill Vintcent?

Have you heard of Nevill Vintcent and his inspiring story? But before we start with the tale, a brief preface. The best introduction to him is contained in the words of J.R.D. Tata, who called him 'undoubtedly the founder of Indian air transport'.

If you prefer a more graphic introduction, here are J.R.D.'s words: 'Nevill Vintcent, that gallant and immensely able man, who conceived the [Tata Airlines] project and managed it with zest and efficiency, until he was shot down over the Atlantic ten years later, on a dangerous flight back to India.'

He was a tall, huge British man of South African origin with blond hair and blue eyes and a burning passion for flying. Apropos of his size, he was also a champion boxer. Born in 1902, he served briefly during World War I and was then commissioned by the Royal Air Force at the age of twenty, where he was honoured for his exceptional courage. Once, piloting a fighter biplane with only a navigator to keep him company, he had to make a forced landing in the Arabian Desert. Hostile Arabian horsemen immediately rushed at the plane to capture both its occupants. Vintcent quickly got out, lifted the rear of the aircraft, put it on his shoulder and turned it around manually so that the navigator could use the mounted gun (aircraft in those days had a single fixed machine gun) to fire at the Arab tribesmen. They dispersed immediately.

How did this man become co-founder of air transport in India alongside J.R.D. Tata? That exciting voyage started when Vintcent came to India in the late 1920s, along with a colleague in his de Havilland aircraft. After World War I ended, he had flown airmail between Borneo and the Straits settlements and become convinced that India had huge potential for commercial aviation. In Mumbai, he first contacted Russa Mehta, the son of textile industrialist Sir Homi Mehta with his proposal to start an airline. But he did not get a positive response there. His next port of call was J.R.D. Tata, who had, coincidentally, just received his own pilot's licence.

J.R.D. and Nevill first met in 1929. Vintcent's plan for a commercial airline in India appears to have resonated with the young J.R.D. As they discussed the proposal, J.R.D. appears to have quickly developed the conviction that India needed an airline for its future, and also the business potential of such an enterprise. But most of all, he was struck by Vintcent's great passion, knowledge and ability. Perhaps he also saw in him the entrepreneurial streak which is required to build a new enterprise.

So J.R.D. requested Vintcent to submit a business proposal, which he took up to Sir Dorabji Tata, the then chairman of the Tata Group. After some hesitation, and reassured by the fact that the initial investment required was only Rs 2 lakh, Sir Dorab agreed. The Tatas wrote to the British Government of India, seeking their support and approval for commencing an airline in the country.

That led to a great amount of protracted correspondence for the next three years. Initially, the Tatas requested a subsidy, which was rejected. Then, there was a lot of dilly-dallying by the government, which was probably not keen to permit an Indian firm to start an airline. J.R.D. Tata and his chairman, Sir Dorabji Tata, were getting increasingly restless, even frustrated, at the various impediments being put in their path.

But Vintcent was a determined young man who would not let government bureaucracy come in his way, particularly because he was convinced that the Tata business proposal was in the interests of the country. He decided to take forward the conversation directly with the viceroy, Lord Willingdon, and went all the way to Simla to seek a meeting with him. Writing to J.R.D. from Simla on 20 May 1931, he says: 'Yesterday, I lunched at the Viceregal Lodge and managed to get about ten minutes' conversation with H.E. [Lord Willingdon], and told him briefly about the situation . . . I asked him whether in his opinion Indian firms should be encouraged to engage in air transport, and he said most emphatically that he was in favour of it . . . I shall try to interest him further so that he may let his opinion be known.'

It took many more months before the government eventually approved the Tata Airlines proposal. A ten-year contract for carrying airmail was eventually signed between the Tata Group and the Government of India on 24 April 1932. Soon, for J.R.D. Tata, Nevill Vintcent became the expert sounding board and guide in all aspects of establishing this airline, including the type of aircraft and the operating expenses involved.

On 15 October 1932, the inaugural flight of the Tata Aviation Service took off from Karachi to Mumbai, piloted by J.R.D. Tata himself. J.R.D. the pilot 'soared joyfully from Karachi with our first precious load of mail'. After a refuelling stop at Ahmedabad, he landed in Mumbai at 1.50 p.m. and delivered to the postmaster 55 pounds of mail meant for the city. This was a proud day for India with its first-ever commercial flight.

On this occasion, too, Vintcent was J.R.D.'s close collaborator. He received J.R.D. at the Mumbai airport, and, within twenty minutes, took off with mail destined for Madras with a halt en route at the town of Bellary (which also received 6 pounds of mail). This then became a weekly feature, the Tata airmail flight from Karachi to Madras via Mumbai and Bellary.

Thanks to J.R.D.'s passion for excellence and Vintcent's strong operational capabilities in aviation, the airline completed its first year with a perfect 100 per cent punctuality record. The Directorate General of Civil Aviation, in its report for 1933–34, said, 'As an example of how an airmail service should be run, we commend the efficiency of Tata Services . . . Imperial Airways might send their staff on deputation to Tatas to see how it is done.'

The airline flourished and its profits rose substantially. Soon, the airline was carrying both passengers and mail. It was operated with great discipline and efficiency, and in 1939, a passenger could fly from Bombay to Delhi at slightly less than the first-class rail fare!

However, with the outbreak of World War II towards the end of 1939, civil aviation was suspended in India. The Tata aircraft were put at the government's command, where they rendered exceptional service to the Royal Air Force (RAF), including transporting wounded military personnel and refugees.

During this period, Vintcent would travel with J.R.D. and discuss with him plans for the airline they had founded. When war broke out, Vintcent the entrepreneur immediately saw an opportunity to build an aircraft factory in India. Once again, J.R.D. resonated with this idea because it would provide the country with indigenous aircraft that would be required after the war.

Initially, the British government agreed to support this proposal, though they would later suddenly back out. Vintcent travelled to London in 1942 where he undertook discussions with the British government for the manufacture of the Mosquito aircraft in Indian factories. So enthusiastic was he about putting this idea into action quickly that he wanted to come back to India as soon as possible to firm up details.

This was wartime and the fastest route back was to request a lift in an RAF aircraft. He did so and boarded an RAF Hudson bomber plane on 29 January 1942. Unfortunately, the aircraft disappeared without a trace. There was no news of Nevill Vintcent thereafter. It is said that for some time, J.R.D. Tata kept waiting for his beloved friend and colleague to come back, but he never did.

It soon became clear that the Hudson bomber had been shot down somewhere off the coast of France. Vintcent's body was never discovered, but the sad reality soon dawned on everyone. The man who had helped co-found India's first airline along with J.R.D. had disappeared off the face of the Earth, at the young age of forty.

R.M. Lala, J.R.D. Tata's biographer, narrates a beautiful French quote which J.R.D. would sometimes use: 'When someone dear to us passes away, a part of us dies with him too.' This was clearly the case with J.R.D. Tata and Nevill Vintcent. The two men had associated so closely that their bonds went beyond work alone. They had immersed themselves in creating a new industry for India, commercial aviation, a space that would soon become very important to its future.

It is said that J.R.D. Tata kept a photograph of Vintcent on his worktable, next to a picture of his father. Undoubtedly, Jeh was fond of him, and he also respected him for all his contributions towards creating and nurturing Tata Airlines, which went on to become Air India.

This story is important for two reasons. First, to pay tribute to Nevill Vintcent, who conceptualized India's first commercial airline and then helped J.R.D. Tata establish it. He came from a foreign land with a dream for India and brought his proposal to glorious life. We should not forget him.

Second, to reflect on the nature of professionals such as Vintcent who combine restless entrepreneurship, commitment to excellence and total dedication. Such are the leaders who open and create successful new horizons for any enterprise.

34

People, First and Foremost

Where shall we begin the colourful story of Russi Mody, one of the most endearing corporate leaders of our time?

Let's start with his college days at Oxford University, where he would skip most of his classes, play the piano, and attend all meetings of the students' union, where he thoroughly enjoyed speaking. At Oxford, he also met the legendary scientist Albert Einstein, who played the violin in his leisure time. Both of them ended up playing duets together in Russi's room, and also rendering a few joint public performances of their music.

But the true music of Russi Mody's life began playing out when he joined the Tata Group in 1939. In that year, he joined Tata Steel at Jamshedpur, starting as a *khalasi* (shop-floor trainee) in the coke oven. Russi came from a privileged background, being the son of Sir Homi Mody, a director of the Tata Group and later also governor of the United Provinces. He could perhaps have worked in a plush Tata office in Mumbai or Kolkata. But he asked for an opening in the factory because he fell in love with the town of Jamshedpur, and he also wanted to gain practical experience.

That shop-floor experience perhaps added greatly to his penchant for connecting with ordinary people extraordinarily well. In the 1940s, he had graduated to being a deputy superintendent buying coal for Tata Steel in Kolkata. There, his was the only department whose employees chose not to join a newly formed mercantile union because they were very happy with their boss and therefore saw no need at all for a union. This unusual fact came to J.R.D. Tata's notice. J.R.D. was impressed and moved Russi Mody to a role in the company's personnel department, which had just been formed.

What happened next? Listen to Russi Mody's own narration of this interesting story (extracted from a speech he delivered many years later at the Tata Group headquarters, Bombay House):

About six weeks later, I was coming home one afternoon . . . I suddenly saw people running from the [steel] works, some with bloodstained shirts, some with stab wounds, everybody running helter skelter . . . I walked towards the main gate to find out what was happening . . . before I could realize what had happened, I was in the midst of an angry mob. I had never faced a labour mob in my life. Anyhow, I found them screaming and shouting.

Now, frankly, it was a question of survival . . . My Hindi was practically absent at that time . . . So I said, '*Kya hai? Kya taklif hai?* [What is it? What is the trouble?]' To my surprise, I found them responding to me, saying, '*Saheb, yeh hai, who hai* [Sir, it is this, it is that].' They did not hit me. I was not assaulted. So I kept talking to them . . . I said, '*Bait jao na. Bait kar baat karona* [Please sit down. Speak after sitting down].' To my utter surprise, they sat down.

All that I would say to them was, 'I will personally look into your grievances. If some of you will come and talk to me.' They said, 'You will personally look into it?' I said, 'Yes.'

So they started explaining to me that all throughout the
[World] war, they had been oppressed. Now they were going
to be independent. I said, 'All right. I am independent too.
Let us all get down together and talk about it.'

Russi Mody then listened to those agitating workers patiently,
sitting down and speaking with them, understanding the issues
that had been bottled up within them, for more than an hour.
Then, he asked them to go to work and come back to talk the
next day. Amazingly, they readily agreed and did so. They were
heartened, perhaps even amazed, by the fact that a manager had
decided to sit down with them, right then and there in front of
the gates, and listen to their grievances so openly. To them, first
and foremost, it was a mark of human respect and regard for
their problems.

This was the beginning of a long friendship. Russi Mody
went on to say: 'If you ever experience this very satisfying
experience of being a friend to poorer people, you will have
experienced a far more lasting friendship than generally exists
between people of our own social status.'

Russi's friendship with the workers of Tata Steel was a
lifelong bond. He recognized that happy workers, whose dignity
and self-esteem were respected, would work with enhanced
commitment and dedication to the company. Throughout his
career, he spent enormous energy and time on crafting several
such win-win solutions.

Consider this story. In 1965, now a director, he took charge
of the Ferromanganese plant, which was making significant
losses at that time. The first question he asked was, 'What are
the grievances and what is the morale of the workers?' He then
met all the 450 workers of this plant himself, in batches of fifty,
at the Director's Bungalow. Everyone sat down at this huge
mansion over cold drinks.

Initially, the workers were silent because they had never been met personally in such style by their director. But as the conversation progressed, it became clear that they had two key grievances—lack of appropriate boots, and lack of helmets. Russi Mody approved both these items on the spot, incurring a cost of around Rs 3 lakh. The productivity of the plant skyrocketed in the months and years thereafter, and within two years, it had become profitable.

In 1974, after several successful stints, and thirty-five years after he had first joined Tata Steel as a khalasi, Russi Mody was appointed managing director of the company. Tata Steel achieved excellent business results under his leadership. In 1983, he was chosen as 'Businessman of the Year' by *Business India*. In 1986, BBC featured him as one of the six ace industrial personalities in the world. In 1989, he was conferred the Padma Bhushan by the Government of India.

While he was indeed a very successful business leader of his times, his heart remained with his people, and with the community. His keen interest in tribal (Adivasi) welfare led to one of the most progressive tribal development programmes in the country, which Tata Steel has taken forward wonderfully well over the years. Similarly, rural development was close to his heart, and so was his belief that 'sports is a way of life'. He established the Tata Football Academy in Jamshedpur with the ace Indian footballer Chuni Goswami as its director. Russi was ever at ease with all his people—eating with his workers, conducting relaxed and long town halls with them, attending cultural events with their families, or even spontaneously inviting some of them to drive along with him in his car.

T.R. Doongaji, a retired director of the Tata Group, who was closely associated with Russi Mody, has written: 'Trusting and empowering his people, Russi Mody inspired performance, he did not command it.' J.R.D. Tata has called him 'a remarkable man', and Ratan Tata has referred to him as 'an institution at Tata Steel'.

The final eighteen months of Russi Mody's long tenure at Tata Steel were unfortunately marred by his serious differences with the Tata Group, which led to his exit from Tata Steel in April 1993. This episode has been covered extensively in the Indian media and is not the subject of this tribute. It is, however, a matter of great comfort to everyone who knew Russi that things once again became friendly and fences were mended well before he passed away in 2014 at the ripe old age of ninety-six. The nation, the Tata Group and Tata Steel mourned his demise, even as they paid rich tribute to the memory of a man who was always one with his people.

Russi Mody lived life to the fullest, peppered with a lot of good food, fun and joy. Stories of the sixteen-egg omelettes which he ate are the stuff of legend. He was equally at home in the mines of Noamundi as he was on a yacht in the French Riviera, which he would visit often on his vacations. But wherever he was, there was one mantra that was sacrosanct to him—he insisted on dignity and self-esteem for the employees of his vast company.

Even when he declined a worker's request, he wrote gracefully to him or her. He is known to have signed around 5 lakh letters addressed to employees of Tata Steel. Most of them were letters of regret, and yet workers treasured these letters from their wonderful leader, who always treated them with the utmost respect. In fact, many of them framed the letters and hung them on the walls of their homes.

There cannot be a better tribute to this extraordinary leader of people. His life holds so many invaluable lessons for each of us.

35

The Maharajah Man

This is the delightful story of one of India's first marketing wizards, a maverick of the Tata Group, and a close associate and friend of J.R.D. Tata. He's the man behind the Maharajah, the lovable mascot of Air India: Sorab Kaikushroo Kooka, aka Bobby Kooka.

Bobby Kooka was recruited into the aviation department of the Tata Group in the year 1938. Tata Airlines was still a fledgling airline service at that time. Many years later, J.R.D. Tata fondly narrated the tale of how he first met the man.

'I don't know how many of you there are here tonight who were in Tata Airlines in May 1938—probably not many—when Mr Kooka first burst upon an astonished air transport world which has never been the same since. On that fateful day in May, Mr Kooka appeared in my office and, having pointed out the deficiencies in the Tata organization, explained how badly needed he was in Tatas to put them right . . . I decided that if there was any place for him in Tatas, it could only be in Tata Airlines. Furthermore, in those days, the chances of survival of Tata Airlines were pretty dim and so it was clear that by employing him there we would be taking little risk of making any permanent commitment.'

Bobby Kooka also recalled this first encounter with J.R.D. Tata in his inimitable style: 'I was told that I would have to see Mr J.R.D. Tata. I was warned that Mr Tata was a terror. Heart in mouth, I went to his office. He asked me very searching questions, none of which could I answer. He was obviously impressed, so impressed, that within seconds, I was ushered out of the room . . .'

Driving this banter was a brilliant, fertile marketing brain. After spending a few years as secretary of Tata Airlines, Bobby Kooka had decided to give the brand (now rechristened as Air India, with J.R.D. as chairman) a human face that represented India with charm and dignity. At the first booking office of the company, located in Churchgate in Mumbai, he created 'an oriental potentate, sitting on a magic carpet, smoking a bubble hookah'. This was the beginning of the Air India Maharajah, perhaps India's very own first advertising mascot that went on to win millions of hearts across the world.

In Bobby Kooka's own words: 'We call him a Maharajah for want of a better description. But his blood isn't blue. He might look like royalty, but he isn't royal.' Working together with Umesh Rao of J. Walter Thomson, the advertising agency, Kooka envisioned with flourish such a lovable symbol of India—a round face, with an outsized moustache, striped turban and long nose.

After making his first appearance in 1946, the Maharajah was all over the world, in the process making Air India one of the most visible and engaging brands globally. Fifty years before Google even thought of Google Doodles, Bobby Kooka was constantly reinventing the Maharajah—as a lover boy in Paris, a sumo wrestler in Tokyo, a Romeo in Rome, and a guru of transcendental meditation in Rishikesh. The Maharajah was funny, irreverent, up to antics, but always full of India, his proud homeland. He was a friend to every traveller on India's national airline, and would reach out to them with warmth and hospitality.

Bobby Kooka also extended this 'Indianness' to every office of the airline, worldwide. Imagery, dances, paintings and sculptures from India appeared in the offices of Air India in New York, Geneva and London, making the airline a beautiful showcase of the country's great heritage. This, in turn, attracted many global travellers to make it their airline of choice. The legendary film-maker Muzaffar Ali, who worked as a member of Bobby Kooka's marketing team for many years, said, 'For eleven years, I was on a flight, dreaming through the eyes of Kooka and his mentor J.R.D. I was not working for Air India, but for India.'

What beautiful words. Not only was Kooka a marketing genius, he was also a maverick who created storms in many teacups in his time. He used to write for the *Tata House* magazine, editing the last page, called the 'Tata Patter', under various pen names including 'Pestonjee Pepper', 'Umslopogas' and 'Chief of the Amazulus'. On the page 'Tata Patter', he proceeded to, in the words of J.R.D. Tata, 'play havoc with the whole Tata organization by demolishing the ego and assassinating the character of every Tata director and senior official . . . [also], through Air India hoardings, he demolished and punctured innumerable egos, which placed me at the receiving end of endless complaints from MPs and ministers, including Mr Morarji Desai and Mr Krishna Menon, who were depicted in red pants running a track race with Mr Kripalani.'

But nonetheless, J.R.D. Tata provided Bobby Kooka with the required support throughout his career, because he recognized Kooka's genius, and perhaps also the need for some benign humour in the midst of our daily challenges. As J.R.D. said at

Bobby Kooka's retirement function in 1971: 'May you never cease tilting at windmills, at the pretentious, the charlatans, and the hypocrites of the world.' He also said, 'I forgive him all the apologies I had to tender on his behalf. I forgive him all the scars that I have borne because of the pleasure, the laughter and the relief from frustration and boredom that he provided to thousands, and perhaps millions, of people.'

This immediately reminds me of one of J.R.D. Tata's key secrets to his success, of which he says, 'If I have any merit, it is getting on with individuals according to their ways and characteristics . . . to be a leader, you have to lead human beings with affection.' J.R.D. led the maverick Bobby Kooka with that same human affection, and, in turn, Kooka led the fabulously successful marketing and publicity efforts for the nation's flagship airline, including the creation and nurturing of the Air India Maharajah.

36

Why Did Jamsetji Tata Build the Taj?

On one fine day in 1898, Jamsetji Tata, founder of the Tata Group, suddenly announced that he would build a grand hotel in Mumbai. He said he had bought out the lease of a large plot in the Apollo Bunder area of the city from the Port Trust specifically for this hotel.

This announcement took everyone by complete surprise. Even his closest business associates did not know that such a venture was on its way. By then, Jamsetji Tata was already a prosperous businessman who had established successful textile mills. He was also one of Mumbai's most progressive property owners. He had already announced his vision of creating India's first integrated steel plant and the country's first hydroelectric venture. But a hotel? Here was a successful industrialist; what did he know about being a hotelier?

It is said that when he announced this grand new venture to his family, his sisters were taken aback. One of them is said to have replied, in Gujarati: 'What?? You are building an institute of science in Bangalore, a great iron and steel factory, and a hydroelectric project—and now you tell us you are going to put up a *bhatarkhana* [eating house]!'

Today, more than a century later, we know the Taj Mahal Hotel in Mumbai as India's finest luxury hotel. Taj is an immensely successful hotel, and 'Tajness' is Indian hospitality at its best. The legendary actor Gregory Peck called this hotel a 'jewelled crown'. It has played gracious host to presidents, royalty and rock stars. It has survived two World Wars, as well as a ghastly terrorist attack in 2008, and it has taken glorious rebirth. Indeed, more than just a hotel, the Taj epitomizes the spirit of Mumbai and India.

But the old mystery remains—why did Jamsetji Tata build the Taj? Why did he so suddenly lease out two and a quarter acres of land from the Bombay Port Trust and then invest a huge amount in building this hotel? Indeed, what was it that had been growing in his thoughts for so long that it prompted such an audacious decision?

A popular and apocryphal story that has made the rounds over the years is that Jamsetji Tata wanted to create the Taj Mahal Hotel because he was refused admission to the Watson's Hotel in Mumbai since he was not European and the hotel did not admit Indians. Therefore, he wanted to build a grand hotel that could be used by Indians and Europeans alike. This story is almost certainly untrue even though such discrimination based on race may well have existed in those days. In fact, the historians Sharada Dwivedi and Charles Allen have said that this 'seems far too petty a reason to fire a man of the calibre of J.N. Tata, who in the past had not hesitated to cross swords with governments and petty commercial combines'.

In that case, could the desire to build a large hotel business have been the primary motivation for building the Taj? After all, Jamsetji Tata was constantly driven by a restless desire to expand his business ventures. But this also was clearly not the reason because Jamsetji had no desire to run a hotel company. In fact, he had hoped to dispose of the lease of the hotel to a European company, but unfortunately, the negotiations fell through. And that's how he found himself handling the hotel.

A third possible reason could have been the desire to gain significant financial returns from this investment in a hotel. Indeed, this is a legitimate goal for any business person to pursue. But in this specific case, this appears untrue too. Consider the facts for a moment. Jamsetji Tata's prospectus for the hotel talked of first-class restaurants, grand suites, India's first Turkish bath and the first commercial building in Mumbai to be lit with electric lights. He also went on a global buying spree for the hotel, across London, Dusseldorf, Berlin and Paris, sparing no cost to equip it with the finest infrastructure and accessories—a carbon dioxide ice-making plant to provide India's first cooling system for hotel rooms, German lift machinery, American fans and spun steel pillars from Paris for the ballroom of the hotel. All this cost enormous sums of money, eventually pushing up his investment to Rs 26 lakh, a stupendous figure in those days.

When the Taj Mahal Hotel opened its doors in 1903, rooms were priced starting at a 'moderate' Rs 6 per day—which was perhaps the competitive room rate for those times. Yet it opened with only seventeen guests. Clearly, if significant financial returns had to be earned in the near future, building such a grand and lavishly appointed hotel was not the answer. In fact, the hotel and its expenditure posed a risk to his overall earnings, and some of his contemporaries called it 'Tata's white elephant'.

This brings us to what is perhaps the only plausible reason for Jamsetji Tata's burning desire to build the Taj—his love for his home town, Mumbai, and his belief that a very good hotel was essential for the city to attract visitors and develop further. While there are no letters or documents written by Jamsetji himself in this regard, notes maintained by his personal assistant A.J. Bilimoria (and quoted by Jamsetji's chronicler, Frank Harris) are revealing. One of these notes says:

> As he believed that the installation of an up-to-date hotel in Bombay was one of the essential conditions of the city's advancement, and that no other capitalist was likely to venture, he considered it was his duty to provide the want.

Similarly, a friend of Jamsetji Tata, Lovat Fraser, who served as editor of the *Times of India* in Mumbai, said, 'He [Jamsetji Tata] came to me and told me that the idea had long been simmering in his mind, and that he had made much study of the subject. He had not the slightest desire to own a hotel, however; his sole wish was to attract people to India, and incidentally to improve Mumbai.'

At that time, Mumbai did not have a first-class hotel that could place it anywhere among the top cities in the world, that would attract people to come and visit or stay. In fact, the city's *Saturday Review* had lamented in 1865: 'When will Bombay have a rest house worthy of the name?' Jamsetji Tata himself had travelled extensively to Europe and America, and he had seen for himself the comforts available to travellers in those countries. This had perhaps further fuelled his love for Mumbai and the reputation of his city and nation.

What made matters worse is that in 1897, just one year before Jamsetji announced his desire to build the Taj, Mumbai had been ravaged by the bubonic plague. There was death everywhere and mortality rates reached 1900 deaths every week that year. Large numbers of people had left the city, industries had closed down, and business confidence had plummeted. Now, in addition to medical treatment and inoculation, which was already in play, this great city, the commercial capital of India, also desperately needed grand symbols of recovery to get up and walk and, very importantly, to get back its pride.

Jamsetji Tata must have been driven by this factor too— wanting to create a grand hotel which would present a superb new image of a reconstructed Mumbai to the world at large. The historians Sharada Dwivedi and Charles Allen have discussed this in greater detail in their excellent coffee-table book *The Taj at Apollo Bunder*.

So, at the heart of it all, the reason why Jamsetji Tata built the Taj Mahal Hotel was his love for Mumbai and India. For him, the 'why' was so powerful that it urged him to stake his reputation, withstand all scepticism, and invest a very large sum of resources to create the iconic hotel. When the 'why' is powerful enough, the what and the how eventually reveal themselves to us, and are fulfilled in many ways. And particularly because we live life but once, figuring out our own 'why' is so important to unlocking the power of our lives.

37

Never Stop Dreaming

Jamsetji Tata, founder of the Tata Group, is known for establishing very successful, pioneering business ventures that have gone on to shape Indian industry. But did you know that the tale of his life is also the story of a man who never ever stopped dreaming?

During the first three decades after founding the Tata Group in 1868, Jamsetji had already established very successful textile mills—Empress Mills in Nagpur, Swadeshi Mills in Mumbai and Advance Mills in Ahmedabad. He had conceptualized India's first integrated steel plant in Jamshedpur, which would bloom into Tata Steel. He had planned the country's most ambitious hydroelectric power plant at Walwhan on the Western Ghats and had begun working towards establishing the fabulous Taj Mahal Hotel in Mumbai. He had even embarked on creating India's first full-fledged science research university, the Indian Institute of Science, at Bangalore, and launched the country's first scholarships for higher education overseas for Indians.

Put together, these pioneering and ambitious ventures make for the story of a complete and fulfilling life. Surely, their planning and execution must have kept Jamsetji Tata substantially preoccupied. Indeed, one of his early biographers wrote: 'Had he no other title to recognition, his conduct of the mills would suffice.' But all this did not stop him from dreaming about many other possibilities for his beloved nation.

One of his most imaginative projects centred on creating adequate cold storage for the city of Mumbai. He wanted to increase the food supply and prevent constant shortages in the period immediately after the devastating bubonic plague of the 1890s by setting up a cold storage plant for fruits and fish. Therefore, around 1900, he began drawing up plans for a huge building to be constructed on the land that is now occupied by the Chhatrapati Shivaji Maharaj Vastu Sangrahalaya (earlier called the Prince of Wales Museum).

This was to be a circular building surrounding a huge house of ice where the manufacture of artificial ice would cool the entire structure. The external perimeter of the building would contain offices that could be leased out, or even rooms for concerts, all of which would be suitably 'air-conditioned' by the central ice-house. Jamsetji's dream was evidently ahead of its time and this project would not come to fruition in his lifetime. It would take another twenty years before his dream was realized, albeit in a different format, when the iconic Crawford Market in Mumbai became equipped with adequate cold storage and refrigerators.

Another dream that Jamsetji pursued with passion was the establishment of India's own shipping line. He believed that a country which depends on the ships of another nation faces a permanent disadvantage. He also resented the exorbitant charges on the transport of Indian cotton yarn levied by the British-owned Peninsular and Oriental (P&O) line, which held a monopoly on shipping out of India in those days. So, he travelled to Japan and after reaching an agreement with the well-established Nippon Yusen Kaisha (NYK) line, he established the Tata line, for which he bought two ships, *Annie Barrow* and *Lindisfarne*, which would carry Indian cotton goods and yarn, alongside the Japanese ships of NYK, at reasonable freight charges.

The Indian media commended the courage of Jamsetji in trying to break a huge monopoly. Soon, however, the P&O line, which was subsidized by the revenues and taxpayers of India, decided to safeguard their monopoly and ruthlessly crush all competition by reducing rates to hugely unviable levels. They even made the unusual offer of carrying Indian cotton to Japan free of charge if shippers signed suitable declarations with them. Jamsetji Tata took up this matter strongly and repeatedly with the Secretary of State for India in the British government but to no avail. The cotton mills of Mumbai gradually withdrew their contracts from the Tata line. So, the two ships were sent back to England, and the relatively small Tata line shut down. However, the venture did help Japan's NYK get an initial foothold in the Indian market, which eventually created some degree of competition, to the benefit of Indian manufacturers and merchants.

This reversal did not stop Jamsetji from pursuing other equally ambitious dreams. At Bangalore, he created a silk farm to implement in India many of the scientific principles of sericulture, which he had seen in Japan, and therefore, he also created the required skillsets in the country. The Tata Silk Farm was quite a successful venture. While the farm no longer exists, back then it provided the impetus for the revival of the local silk industry. Some of the giants of Indian sericulture, such as Appadorai Mudaliar and Laxman Rao, were amongst the Tata Silk Farm's first trainees. Many years later, in 1949, the Central Silk Board was also established in Bangalore.

Yet another dream was the desire to encourage the growth of Egyptian cotton in India. Here, the intent in Jamsetji Tata's mind was to help Indian mills spin yarn of finer counts, for which Egyptian cotton was eminently suitable. He studied this subject in detail and was concerned that countries like Germany, Austria, Belgium and England were flooding the Indian market with their manufactured cotton goods. Therefore, in a rallying cry, he implored all Indians to save India's 'young and only' industry from utter destruction. He passionately argued: 'If India were enabled to grow for itself the long-stapled varieties, she would derive immense benefit in three different directions— such an expansion would assist agriculture, conserve the money of the country, and improve the exchange.'

Experiments to grow Egyptian cotton in India began in right earnest. In some districts in the central provinces, these ventures achieved success, whereas, in many other places, they failed. This was already the twilight of Jamsetji Tata's life; he was deeply immersed in his steel, hydroelectric, hotel and science education ventures, and he eventually concluded that from a cost–benefit standpoint, it would not be advisable to give further attention to this project.

Jamsetji's capacity to dream remained with him until the very end. The last days of his life were spent in Europe consulting expert doctors. Although still robust in spirit, his heart had grown weak, and he suffered from sleeplessness and immense breathing difficulties. So, in San Remo, Italy, on an occasional good day, he would go to the marketplace and buy fresh fruits, something he loved eating. There, he began to dream of cultivating dates and other Mediterranean fruits in India, given their nutritious content. A few days later, he passed away, warmly ensconced in the love of his family. We do not know what his final dream was, but there can be no doubt that it must have been a dream that brought alive his deep love for India, the nation that he worked for and championed throughout his life.

Never stop dreaming. Dreams are the visions that help unfold and enrich our lives. Despite having created such pioneering and successful businesses, and notwithstanding many challenges and a few failures too, Jamsetji Tata never stopped dreaming throughout his life. Why should we?

38

An Eagle Takes to the Skies

It is well known that J.R.D. Tata was fond of flying, but he also wanted India's future leaders to soar high in the intellectual skies, as eagles do. This is the story of a unique institution that he helped establish in pursuit of this goal.

In March 1964, speaking at the Indian Institute of Science, Bangalore, J.R.D. emphasized the need to start a very different type of academic institution 'for the most talented' young Indians who could grow to leadership positions. In essence, he was reflecting upon the need for these young people to be trained not merely in the scientific spirit or in the humanistic arts, but in a rigorous combination of both worlds.

J.R.D. was a great admirer of the education system in France, and the benchmark in his mind was the French *grande écoles*. He was impressed that over 70 per cent of the top jobs in the French Civil Service and scientific institutions were occupied by graduates of these excellent institutions, which trained their students not merely in technical subjects, but also in 'exceptionally severe moral and intellectual disciplines'. Hence, the young leaders emerging from the grande écoles were well-rounded people with both depth and breadth of knowledge across fields as diverse as mathematics, psychology, history and sociology. This range of learning helped enormously as they progressed towards positions of decision-making.

On 1 July 1964, J.R.D. wrote to Indira Gandhi, suggesting that such an institution could be created as a memorial to the late Jawaharlal Nehru, who had passed away earlier that year. He suggested that the project be undertaken by the Nehru Memorial Trust, with significant contribution from the Tata Group as well.

J.R.D. was duly called to a meeting of the Nehru Memorial Trust, which was chaired by Indira Gandhi, to discuss this proposal. Dr Karan Singh, the former prince regent and governor of Jammu and Kashmir, and now minister of aviation, was the secretary of this trust. J.R.D. went armed with the report of a detailed study led by the French professor John Capelle, who was, at that time, the director general of education in Paris. The professor and an expert committee had examined what such an institution in India should look like. One of the points he had made was that Indian students should have a good grounding in mathematics, just as it was in the grande écoles, because the study of maths led to clarity of deep thought, logic and rigour in analysis.

Dr Karan Singh, who was a scholar, poet and philosopher, took serious objection to this particular point. J.R.D. Tata has narrated this interesting episode in a speech which he delivered many years later when the institute was eventually inaugurated:

Karan Singh said to me: 'Jeh, what is this nonsense about mathematics? Do you mean to say that if this school of yours had been there when I was a college student, I would not have been admitted?'

All I could say was: 'Well, Karan, if you were as poor at mathematics as I was, then neither you nor I would have been admitted.'

Dr Karan Singh did not take this too well. He threw the brochure on the table and said, 'Nonsense.' As a result of which the proposal was summarily rejected.

So, unfortunately, the idea got dropped at the time. J.R.D. was undoubtedly upset but he was a determined man. Nearly twenty years later, in the early 1980s, he brought up the idea once again. By now, India had established its own Indian Institutes of Technology (IITs) and Management (IIMs), which were fast becoming world-class.

However, the need for rigorous, multidisciplinary higher education, combining the sciences and the humanities, was still very relevant, particularly as continuing education for experienced professionals who were ready to make the leap to leadership positions. As many of us in the corporate world may have realized, being either engineer-MBAs, chartered accountants or liberal arts graduates does not necessarily give us the sheer breadth of perspective required for three to four decades of our careers.

Once again, in 1984, J.R.D. Tata established a working group to consider this unique idea. He invited Professor Olmer from the Ministry of Education in Paris. He also invited some of India's leading intellectuals—Professor M.G.K. Menon, Professor Satish Pradhan, Dr L.K. Jha, Dr H.N. Sethna and Professor Rustum Choksi—to be members.

This working group recommended an institute of continuing education, which would go well beyond the IITs and IIMs. It would provide the intellectual rigour and joy of multidisciplinary education to mid-career professionals poised for leadership. These people may be exceedingly talented in their own narrow fields, but the new breadth of knowledge would help them achieve future breakthroughs for their institutions and the nation at large.

Based on this recommendation, the National Institute of Advanced Studies (NIAS) was eventually established in 1988. It was located within the campus of the Indian Institute of Science (IISc), Bangalore, which itself had been established by Jamsetji Tata, founder of the Tata Group, nearly eighty years earlier. In many ways, NIAS is a sister institute to IISc, and perhaps also evokes Jamsetji's original vision that 'humanities' are as important as the 'sciences' to raise the quality of life of the community. Just like IISc, NIAS does not carry the Tata name as they are both dedicated to the nation.

This time around, J.R.D. ensured that the proposal did not falter because of diverse views by the powers that be. He did so by ensuring initial funding of the project by the Sir Dorabji Tata Trust. Thereafter, other companies of the Tata Group, such as Tata Steel, Tata Motors (TELCO) and Tata Chemicals, also provided early grants.

Quite fittingly for an institute of multidisciplinary education, the first director was Dr Raja Ramanna, one of India's most versatile minds. He had been chairman of the Atomic Energy Commission and had done outstanding research in nuclear physics, but he was also a gifted pianist and had authored books on the structure of music in ragas and Western musical systems.

Some of India's finest intellectuals have taught at NIAS, and many of the multidisciplinary areas of research conducted here are fascinating. NIAS now also offers a coveted doctoral programme. Most recently, in 2017, a Centre for Spatial Analytics and Advanced GIS was established here with support from the Tata Trusts to bring the power of knowledge and science to a wide range of societal issues, including agriculture and nutrition.

It is this power of knowledge that is reflected in NIAS's emblem. Designed by the renowned Indian sculptor Balan Nambiar, this logo has its roots in a remarkable ancient Sanskrit work called the *Sulva Sutras*, composed before the sixth century BCE. Using deep knowledge of geometry, it portrays how bricks can optimally be arranged for the creation of an altar. Interestingly, the altar has the distinct shape of a falcon or eagle, which also represents knowledge and imagination soaring into the skies—the objective of this unique institution.

Two aspects of this story have fascinated me. First, despite all his corporate commitments as chairman of the Tata Group, J.R.D. Tata found and dedicated time to the subject of multidisciplinary education because he passionately believed that this was important for his beloved country. Second, despite facing resistance and even rejection in his first attempt at creating this institution, he displayed both patience and resilience to make it happen over twenty years later.

Belief, resilience and perseverance are some of the finest human qualities that each of us can aspire for in our own lives.

39

The Last Days of Jamsetji Tata

Jamsetji Tata, who founded the Tata Group in 1868, was a man of exceptional energy. By 1903, he had already laid the foundations for several enterprises of national importance.

He had grown a very successful textiles business, starting with Empress Mills at Nagpur. He had put in place the blueprint for a world-class integrated steel plant for India at Jamshedpur. He had planned clean electric energy for his city of Mumbai through an ambitious hydroelectric project. In 1892, he had founded an endowment for the education abroad of promising Indian students, the first of its kind. Thereafter, he had invested significant effort in evangelizing the country's need for a university of higher education and research in science. And, in 1903, the famous Taj Mahal Hotel in Mumbai, created by him, the finest hotel in the East, had opened its glistening doors.

Jamsetji was consumed with his love for India, which drove these path-breaking enterprises. He rarely rested, and except on Sundays, his work at Tata Sons never stopped. If there was an additional holiday, he would go to the office and sit alone there to think deeply and work. In the mornings, he walked on the seafront, and thereafter read or wrote, until he went to his office. In the evenings, post dinner at home, he engaged once again in reading, which he pursued both for knowledge and pleasure. He was a voracious reader, always wanting to acquire deep knowledge of subjects in which he developed an interest.

He also travelled extensively across the world, in pursuit of his goals. Consider the year 1902. In the course of this single year, he visited the United States of America twice in connection with the steel project. He visited the Niagara Falls to study hydroelectric generation. He travelled to Dusseldorf in Germany to participate in the industrial exhibition there, and also to finalize purchases of German electric generators and lifts required for the Taj Mahal Hotel. In addition, he met, in London, the Secretary of State for India to put forward to him details of all his major projects, including plans for the Indian Institute of Science. Since he happened to be in London on Navroz, Parsi New Year's Day, he also hosted all the Parsis of London, around a hundred of them, for a grand New Year's dinner and cruise on the Thames River. All these travels and activities outside India entailed long and arduous journeys by ship, road or rail, required huge amounts of energy, and took up nearly eight months of that year.

At the age of sixty, perhaps driven by his relentless work and travel, Jamsetji's health began to falter. He often faced difficulty in climbing stairs or getting down from his carriage, but he still insisted on doing both by himself. By the age of sixty-five, he was suffering from sleeplessness and a weak heart. But he resisted the constraints that his doctors had placed on him. He continued to eat well—good food was perhaps his one indulgence—and work hard.

Eventually, his family persuaded him to travel to Egypt, hoping that a change in climate would do him good. During this voyage, he received news that his wife had suddenly passed away. Within a few days of hearing this news, Jamsetji, weak as he was, decided to pay tribute to his wife's memory by pledging a significant amount to create a fund for midwives in his native town of Navsari.

Jamsetji's physical condition continued to deteriorate and his sons then took him to consult a famous Viennese doctor in Europe. There, he had some occasional bursts of good health. So obsessed was he with the purpose for which he lived that during one of these periods he even began working on an ambitious new plan for growing nutritious dates in India. When his cousin R.D. Tata (father of J.R.D. Tata) told Jamsetji that he had already brought great honour to his family name, he replied in his characteristic style: 'If you cannot make it greater, at least preserve it. Do not let things slide. Go on doing our work, and increasing it, but if you cannot, do not lose what we have already done.'

By early 1904, now under treatment in Bad Nauheim in Germany, Jamsetji knew that he was dying. He thanked the Almighty for having provided him with a fulfilling life. On 17 May, even as he was sinking, he cried out for his elder son, Dorab. When Sir Dorabji Tata and his wife Lady Meherbai Tata arrived at his bedside, he spoke affectionately to his daughter-in-law and gently stroked his son's cheek. The next morning, nestled within his loving family, he gently breathed his last.

Upon that marvellous ship that moves into the waters of the beyond, God then carried away this great man, who had given his entire life for his beloved nation. His remains were interred at the Brookwood Cemetery in England, in a mausoleum built in the Persian style.

India mourned its beloved son. There were rich tributes from across the world. Lord Curzon, the British viceroy, said: 'No Indian of the present generation had done more for the commerce and industry of India.'

The *Times of India* wrote about him: 'He was above all a patriot, who made no public speeches. To his mind, wealth, and the industry which led to wealth, were not ends in themselves, but means to an end, the stimulation of the latent resources of the country and its elevation in the scale of nations.'

A few years later, Lord Sydenham, governor of Bombay, quoted this timeless tribute to Jamsetji Tata: 'Wealth came to him in full measure, but he remained to the last what he was by nature, a simple, modest gentleman, seeking neither title or place, and loving with a love that knew no bounds, the country that gave him birth.'

Jamsetji Tata's vision continues to guide the Tata Group until this day. His life should inspire each of us to contribute our best to our community and nation.

40

A Legend with a Heart of Gold*

In 1993, I was a thirty-year-old deputy manager at Tata Tea, Bangalore. One morning, I got a call from the managing director's office in Kolkata. Darbari Seth, chairman of the company, wanted to meet me during his forthcoming visit to the tea plantations in Munnar.

Darbari Seth, seventy-three years old by then, was already a legend. He had built Tata Chemicals into a very successful company despite all the odds. Then, he had launched Tata Salt, already a rapidly growing brand. He had negotiated with the Scottish company James Finlay and bought Tata Tea from them for a nominal price. He was also chairman of Tata Coffee and Rallis India. With his broad frame, flowing mane of white hair and sharp eyes, he was a very imposing figure. So all said and done, I was a little scared to meet him.

I met him at Ladbroke House, the Director's Bungalow in Munnar. He asked me to sit down, offered me a cup of tea, put

---

* This is the author's personal tribute to Darbari Seth, a legend of the Tata Group.

me at ease, and then gently asked me whether I would consider moving to Mumbai to work as his executive assistant. I jumped at this opportunity to work with a legend. 'Yes, sir,' I responded quickly. And for the next several months, this stint became, for me, the learning of a lifetime.

Here are a few memorable stories that have stayed on in my mind ever since.

Lots to Do, and Little Time to Lose

At that time, Darbari Seth was working on a very important growth project for the company. This involved a few visits to London for meetings with senior executives of another global company. Sometimes, I would be asked to accompany him, and help out with these meetings as well as the follow-up action thereafter. On one such visit when the meetings were very intense, eventually, both he and I travelled back to Mumbai on the same Air India flight. We landed at Sahar Airport at midnight, and it was around 2.30 a.m. when I got to my home in Colaba. I was dead tired, and slept almost immediately.

Suddenly, at 6 a.m. the next morning, even before the sun had risen fully, the doorbell rang. My wife, Veena, came rushing to our bedroom, woke me up, and said that the chairman's driver had come to meet me. The driver handed over a letter that Darbari Seth had addressed to me. The letter was written in his own handwriting, and contained eight thoughtful points from our London meeting that needed immediate action. And the letter ended with the words: 'We have lots to do, and little time to lose. I will see you in office at 8 a.m.'

Clearly, despite his relatively advanced age, and even after a long international flight, he had sat up at night for at least an hour and written this detailed letter, driven by the urgency and importance of the business at hand. Whereas I, a young boy, was struggling to get out of bed. This work ethic has stayed in my mind ever since. He was deeply committed to his work and immersed himself in it with all the stamina that he could muster.

Tale of the Burnt Toast

On another visit to London, Darbari Seth invited me to stay with him in his apartment at the Taj Hotel, 51, Buckingham Place. This was a two-bedroom apartment with a living room and kitchenette. Early in the morning, I would prepare a nice cup of tea for both of us (he loved masala chai), and he would then read through all the newspapers, preparing for the busy day ahead. One morning, he had an early, important-looking business visitor who came in at 8.30 a.m. Both of them sat in the living room poring over some important papers and blueprints and engaged in official discussions.

Meanwhile, I went into the kitchen to make some breakfast for myself. I still recall vividly, I had decided to eat toast and cheese, along with a banana and some tea. I was watching the tea boil when I noticed thick smoke emanating from the toaster. The toast was almost on fire. It was so badly burnt that the dark smoke quickly enveloped the entire kitchen, setting off the smoke alarm. Smoke must have entered the adjacent living room too, where Darbari Seth was busy in his meeting. I quickly shut the door of the kitchen, but the alarm was shrill enough for everyone to hear. Eventually, someone from the hotel came up, rectified matters, and the smoke gradually dissipated.

Later that morning, as we drove into the city of London for a meeting, I expected Darbari Seth to take up this matter with me strongly enough, because the smoke must have caused serious problems for his important guest and himself. I was mortified. But he did not speak a word of it. Not on that day, and not ever thereafter. Clearly, he knew I had done something wrong in the kitchen, which had created all that smoke, and set off the alarm and the related ruckus. And I was sure he knew because of the way he had smiled at me, with a twinkle in his eyes. Yet, by keeping silent, he had made a more powerful point than he could ever have done by pulling me up.

Dinner at the Chambers

One evening, Darbari Seth hosted an official dinner at the Chambers in the Taj Mahal Hotel, Mumbai, for a visiting minister from Sri Lanka. Since the minister was accompanied by his daughter, I was invited to this event along with my wife. Also present were Dr Manu Seth, the then chief operating officer of the company, and his wife.

This was the first-ever visit to the Chambers for my wife and me, which is perhaps the most exclusive club not just at the Taj but in the entire city. Darbari Seth must have sensed that my wife was feeling a little lost in that extravagant luxury, so he invited her to sit next to him at the table, and advised her that she should let him know what she would like to eat. Then, when the dinner meeting was nearly concluded, he turned again to her and asked her whether she had eaten dessert (it was delicious milk and saffron rabri), and whether she would like a second helping. In fact, he then called upon the white-gloved butler to bring her a special helping of the dessert.

My wife, Veena, who was then a junior engineer at Tata Consultancy Services, remembers that warm gesture even now. 'He was chairman, and I was just a young woman, a junior software engineer. He need not have inquired. The care that he displayed to ensure that I felt comfortable—it made all the difference.'

'Keen to See Your Daughter'

Two years later, in 1995, I had completed my stint as Darbari Seth's executive assistant and had returned to my sales and marketing role in Tata Tea, Bangalore. In May 1995, my wife and I were blessed with our first daughter. I wrote to Darbari Seth, and he promptly wrote back, conveying his congratulations and blessings to the baby. I thought the matter had ended there.

However, a few months later, I had a call from an executive in Tata Coffee. 'Our chairman is in our plantations at Coorg today, and he is driving down to Bangalore this morning. He is keen to see your daughter. Can he reach your home by around 3 p.m.?'

I was delighted and apprehensive and was caught completely off guard. I rushed home from the office. My wife and I spruced up our living room as much as we could. We dressed up my daughter in one of her best little frocks.

At 3 p.m. that afternoon, Darbari Seth reached our home. He was accompanied by a couple of senior officials of Tata Coffee. He sat on our sofa set and asked to hold my daughter in his arms. He smiled at her, kissed her and conveyed his blessings to her personally. He spent around half an hour in our little home, and spoke to my parents as well.

I was truly moved that evening. He chose to do this at the age of seventy-five, after a gruelling drive of five hours from Coorg to Bangalore, and then again in the terrible traffic in Bangalore, all the way to my home at one end of the city. It's amazing how much he cares for people who have worked with him, I thought to myself. I am extremely fortunate to work in a group that has nurtured such legends.

I still cherish two photographs from that beautiful visit. Darbari Seth holding my baby daughter in his arms, and another of him standing happily with our family. So many others who have worked with him have similar stories to narrate. Because, on the one hand, he was a tough taskmaster—and there are many stories of his working relentlessly round the clock with his teams, constantly urging them to ensure that business targets were met and shattered. But on the other hand, he was, for his people, a constant guide and mentor, a powerful leader who cared deeply about them.

Even as we mark his birth centenary in 2020, let us celebrate this remarkable man, technocrat and leader par excellence with a big heart of gold.

Epilogue

Corporate Tales Can Be Bedtime Stories, Too

I wrote the forty Tata stories featured in this book over a period of eight months in 2020, immediately after the coronavirus pandemic burst into our lives, unwelcome and unannounced. The process of research, followed by narration, was intense, enjoyable, immersive and fulfilling. My research partner was Rajendra Prasad Narla, chief archivist at the Tata Central Archives. I wrote the stories steadily, generally at the pace of one each week.

The specific tale that I was in the midst of working on would sometimes appear in my dreams too, during that week. That would make me wonder about my obsession with the history of the Tata Group, and with these stories, and what impact all this may have on me. Nonetheless, I persisted, because this was such an interesting project, and one that connected deeply with me, particularly given my great pride in being a lifelong Tata employee. I was also learning so much about legendary figures from Tata history, the challenges they faced and overcame, and their achievements and dreams, which was rich reward in itself.

Eventually, when each story came to life, I would first post it on the social media platform LinkedIn, where the series soon developed a wide and enthusiastic online readership within the first few weeks. I used the simple hashtag #TataStories to bind the stories together on this platform.

As I published each story, several hundred readers would spontaneously respond with their comments and insights. I am grateful for these responses, because they encouraged me to write even more, and sometimes they also highlighted new story ideas that I could consider. Most readers said they were inspired by these stories. They used beautiful words such as 'pride', 'goosebumps', 'motivation', 'astonishment' and 'joy' to describe their reactions.

One young reader, reflecting on the story of how Jamsetji Tata never stopped dreaming, said, 'These stories help us realize that not everything we dream can materialize, but that should not deter us from dreaming and planning, all over again.'

Another reader called the stories 'nourishing and inspiring'. Yet another reader said about one of them, 'What a stunning story. It inspires me to do a lot more with my own life.'

I was particularly moved by a few readers who told me that some of these were not just corporate stories; they demonstrated timeless, fundamental and powerful values that go into the making of a good human being. Hence, they said, they had begun reading out the stories to their children at bedtime. For instance, a young woman professional wrote a particularly moving letter to me, which said: 'Thank you for bringing Tata Stories to us, I want to let you know how much I have enjoyed reading all of them. It gives me goosebumps, inspires me, brings tears of joy and [is] so inspiring to know such leaders existed and exist . . . Growing up, my father shared some of those stories and made me value the qualities of true leaders. Two years back, my father passed away, he was a businessman who lived his life with honesty. Today, I tell Tata Stories to my four-year-old daughter, who has many questions to ask in each story.'

This was particularly gratifying, because if a mother chooses to read out a Tata story out to her child instead of a fable or a fairy tale, then that says something for the true value of the tale. When I had originally set out to write these Tata stories which would serve as inspiration to people during the particularly challenging time of the pandemic, I must confess that I had not anticipated the deep power they would have to move readers in this extraordinary manner.

Many writers draw strength and motivation from how their readers respond. This was certainly true in my case. Therefore, greatly encouraged by hundreds of these comments and letters, I kept researching and writing with even greater vigour. Several readers suggested that all the stories be compiled into a book, which would help take these narrations to a much wider universe, and also preserve them for future generations to enjoy. That is the genesis of this storybook, and I am thankful that you have taken the time to read it.

I am confident that the future will bring forth many more exciting and meaningful stories from the Tata Group. New tales of adventure and achievement, from fields as diverse as digital transformation, electric vehicles, renewable power, new-age foods and lifestyle products, smart cities, healthcare, enabling livelihoods, evangelizing sports and the fight against the pandemic. Stories of people and places, products and events, but always at their essence, tales of elevating the quality of life of the community, which is at the heart of Tata.

It is also heartening to see, in the recent past, an increasing number of such stories and books from the corporate world at large, and, in particular, from Indian enterprises. Business enterprises have shaped our world in so many ways, and are therefore as much an integral part of modern history as parliaments, presidents and kings. Many iconic corporations worldwide and in India have contributed meaningfully to the progress of society. The stories of how they have accomplished this are the lore of the modern world, and these narratives should be chronicled and celebrated. These stories will also serve to inspire many young people as they prepare to chart out their own lives in a brave new world.

And, of course, if these tales can also serve as charming little bedtime stories for children, then that's a wonderful thing too.

Acknowledgements

The Tata Group and its legends have inspired this book. I feel privileged to have been part of this timeless institution for over three decades now.

I would also like to thank the Tata Group for nurturing the author in me. My sincere gratitude to Ratan Tata, chairman, Tata Trusts, who provided me the opportunity to write my first book, *Tata Log*, eight years ago. That set me off on my writing voyage, and there has been no looking back.

My grateful thanks to N. Chandrasekaran, chairman, Tata Sons, for providing me the support and encouragement to work on this project, and for his gracious words about the book, which I deeply cherish.

R. Gopalakrishnan, retired executive director of Tata Sons, and a prolific author himself, has been my 'writing' mentor. Ever since I began writing my first book, he has generously provided me his time and guidance, which have been invaluable.

This book has only been possible because of the extensive source material provided to me by the Tata Central Archives (TCA), Pune. TCA is a treasure trove of documents, letters, photographs and other historic materials relating to the Tata Group, preserved carefully for posterity.

A special word of thanks for Rajendra Prasad Narla, chief archivist at TCA, who has been my constant partner on this project. Once I outlined to him the broad story or period which I wished to research, he would share with me reams of documents which contained rich and interesting details. He also made the effort to review the stories that I wrote, and his critical observations helped me greatly in giving final shape to the narratives.

I would like to acknowledge the many sources which I have referred to during the writing of this book. These are detailed in the bibliography.

During the course of this project, I received extensive help and inputs from many of my Tata colleagues. Specifically, I would like to convey sincere thanks to T.R. Doongaji, Farokh Subedar, Arun Maira, B.G. Dwarakanath, Michael Foley, Kirti Poonia, Shyamala Ramanan, Atul Agrawal, Sreelakshmi Hariharan and Haroon Bijli, amongst many others.

To Milee Ashwarya and the team at Penguin Random House, thank you for your belief in this book. My conversations with Milee during the early phase of conceptualization and writing were particularly important in clarifying the purpose of this book and developing its framework. Thanks, Milee, for being such a wonderful, supportive friend and guide.

How could I ever have attempted this ambitious project without my editor, Saksham Garg, at my side? The idea of a book such as this took birth during a conversation with Saksham over a glass of red Merlot at a glittering party which Penguin hosted for authors in January 2020 at the Sujan Rajmahal Palace, Jaipur. He then egged me on, provided me guidance on how to make these stories even more engaging, and provoked me into many fresh bouts of thinking. He edited the narrations brilliantly, and also wielded a tight editor's whip, making me rewrite many stories that he was not entirely happy with. I have thoroughly enjoyed working with him, and he has also made me a better writer. Thanks, Saksham, for everything!

To my copy editor, Shreya Chakravertty, I owe thanks for her meticulous work on the text. Her command over the English language, and her instinct for picking absolutely the right word or phrase, is amazing. The stories began to flow so much more seamlessly after she touched them with her magic wand of words.

To my mother, Jayanthi, and my mother-in-law, Vatsala, I thank them for their blessings, which sustain and nourish me. I look forward to gifting them the first two copies of the book.

My daughter, Gayatri, who now lives in New York, has been a constant source of encouragement in all my writing efforts. She is a thoughtful but fierce critic, and I am secretly hoping that this book gets a good review from her.

To my wife, Veena, I want to convey profuse thanks for all her encouragement throughout the research and writing of this book. Much of this effort happened during the peak of the pandemic in 2020, a period when she and I would go out on long walks each evening on garden tracks within the lovely Mumbai apartment complex where we stay. During these daily walks, I would narrate to her the next Tata story that was developing in my mind. She would then critique the story and go on to ask me a few searching questions, which often led to additional thinking and research. She also happily read the first draft of every story and provided me her views. Her love, companionship and support have provided me great strength and motivation at every stage.

I thank God Almighty for blessing me with the passion, capability and constant urge to write. I hope and pray that I can put this wonderful gift to the best possible use throughout my life.

Bibliography

Dear Swami Vivekananda: Part I and II

1. Letter from Jamsetji Tata to Swami Vivekananda, Tata Central Archives, Pune, 23 November 1898.
2. Monthly magazine started by Swami Vivekananda, *Prabuddha Bharata*, Tata Central Archives, Pune, April 1899.
3. Sankari Prasad Basu, 'Vivekananda, Nivedita and Tata's Research Scheme', *Prabuddha Bharata*, October 1978 and November 1978.

OK TATA, OK SUMO

1. Lala, R.M. *Beyond the Last Blue Mountain*. Penguin Books India, 1993, pp. 247–50.
2. Maira, Arun. *The Learning Factory*. Penguin Random House India, 2020.

The Astronaut and the Pioneer

1. *Custodians of the Tata Story*. Tata Central Archives, Pune, 2016, pp. 32–33.

2. Lala, R.M. *Beyond the Last Blue Mountain*. Penguin India, 1993, pp. 177–79.

Tata Indica, India's Own Car

1. Bhat, Harish. *Tata Log*. Penguin India, 2012, pp. 20–49.

Gandhiji in Jamshedpur

1. Note on Mahatma Gandhi's visit to Jamshedpur, Tata Central Archives, Pune, August 1925.
2. Text of Mahatma Gandhi's speech at the TISCO Institute, Tata Central Archives, Pune, August 1925.

A Titan of Our Times

1. Kamath, Vinay. *Titan: Inside India's Most Successful Consumer Brand*. Hachette, 2018, pp. 2–5.

The Creche at Empress Mills

1. Harris, Frank. *Jamsetji Nusserwanji Tata: A Chronicle of His Life*. Blackie & Sons, 1958, pp. 23–46.
2. Speech by Jamsetji Tata at the opening of the new extension of Empress Mills at Nagpur, Tata Central Archives, Pune 1895.

The Tata Silk Farm

1. Harris, Frank. *Jamsetji Nusserwanji Tata: A Chronicle of His Life*. Blackie & Sons, 1958, pp. 103–07.

The Great Dam at Walwhan

1. Harris, Frank. *Jamsetji Nusserwanji Tata: A Chronicle of His Life*. Blackie & Sons, 1958, pp. 219–41.

2. 'Act for Mahseer'. Tata Power: Transforming Lives Stories, https://www.tatapower.com/media/mahseer-matters.aspx.

Tetley and Tata: A Defining Moment

1. Bhat, Harish. *Tata Log*. Penguin India, 2012, pp. 150–73.

Diamonds, Steel and Hearts of Gold

1. Lala, R.M. The Creation of Wealth. Penguin India, 2004, pp. 27–28, 258.
2. *Horizons: The Tata India Century, 1904–2004*. India Book House, 2004, p. 127.
3. Lala, R.M. *Beyond the Last Mountain*. Penguin India, 1993, p. 72.
4. The Jubilee Diamond, https://famousdiamonds.tripod.com/jubileediamond.html
5. 'Diamond Gallery', Mouawad, https://www.mouawad.com/diamonds/diamond-gallery/jubilee.

The Slimmest Watch in the Universe

1. Kamath, Vinay. *Titan: Inside India's Most Successful Consumer Brand*. Hachette, 2018, pp. 145–60.

Coffee, Tea and J.R.D.

1. Kohli, M.S. *JRD: As Air Indians Remember*. Himalayan Books, 2010, p. 8.
2. Lala, R.M. *Beyond the Last Blue Mountain*. Penguin India, 1993, pp. 121–24.
3. Letters of J.R.D. Tata, Tata Central Archives, Pune.

Tata Institute of Fundamental Research

1. Letter from Dr Homi Bhabha to S.D. Saklatwala, Tata Central Archives, Pune, 12 March 1944.
2. Tata Institute of Fundamental Research, archival note prepared by Tata Economic Consultancy Services, Tata Central Archives, Pune.
3. Lala, R.M. *The Creation of Wealth*. Penguin, 2004, pp. 150–56.
4. TIFR. 'History and Vision', https://www.tifr.res.in/portal/history.php.

The Legend of Charles Page Perin

1. Harris, Frank. *Jamsetji Nusserwanji Tata: A Chronicle of His Life*. Blackie & Sons, 1958, pp. 166–67.
2. Lala, R.M. *The Creation of Wealth*. Penguin India, 2004, pp. 21–22.
3. Services, Hungama Digital. 'Tata Steel Campaigns: Jamshedpur At 100: Education', https://www.tatasteel.com/corporate/our-organisation/campaigns/jamshedpurat100/education.

The Fight against Cancer

1. Lala, R.M. *The Creation of Wealth*. Penguin India, 2004, pp. 157–61.
2. *Tata Review*, Vol. 1, No. 1, Tata Central Archives, Pune, April 1965, p. 25.
3. Tata Memorial Hospital, note by Dorabji Tata Trust, Tata Central Archives, Pune, 2 March 1983.

Memorable Letter to a Schoolteacher

1. Letter from J.R.D. Tata to K.C. Bhansali, Tata Central Archives, Pune, 13 September 1965.

League of Tata Scholars

1. Harris, Frank. *Jamsetji Nusserwanji Tata: A Chronicle of His Life*. Blackie & Sons, 1958, pp. 117–18.
2. Agreement dated 7 April 1892, between Jamsetjee Nusserwanjee Tata and Freany K.R. Cama, Tata Central Archives.
3. Contribution of a few eminent J.N. Tata Scholars, Tata Central Archives, Pune.
4. https://www.jntataendowment.org.

The Weavers of Okhai

1. Bhat, Harish. *Tata Log*. Penguin India, 2012, pp. 58–62.
2. 'The Okhai Story', https://okhai.org/pages/the-okhai-story.

Nani Palkhivala: Brilliant Mind, Remarkable Man

1. *Sands of Time*, Special commemorative issue on Nani A. Palkhivala, Tata Central Archives newsletter, Vol. 16, Issue 3, 2020, pp. 1–11.
2. *Business India*, 'The Return of Nani Palkhivala', cover story, September 1979, pp. 3–16.
3. *Horizons: The Tata India Century, 1904–2004*. India Book House, 2004, p. 259.

The Ancient City of Pataliputra

1. Mukherjee, Sraman. 'New Province, Old Capital: Making Patna Pataliputra'. *Indian Economic and Social History Review*, 2009.

Tata and the Olympics

1. Lala, R.M. *Heartbeat of a Trust*. Appendix F, 'Tata and Sports'. McGraw-Hill Publishing Company, 1984.

2. Majumdar, Boria and Mehta, Nalin. *Olympics: The India Story*. '100 Yards Round a Bend to Antwerp: Peasants on the Athletic Track'. HarperCollins, 2012.
3. Pardivala, Jal D. 'Tata Athletes at Home and Abroad'. *Tata Review*, Vol. 7, No. 3, 1972.
4. Indian Olympic Association. 'History', https://olympic.ind. in/ioa-history.
5. *Horizons: The Tata India Century, 1904–2004*. India Book House, 2004, p. 171.

Eka, the Indian Supercomputer

1. Bhat, Harish. *Tata Log*. Penguin India, 2012, pp. 130–49.
2. TOP500. 'November 2007', https://www.top500.org/lists/ top500/2007/11.
3. *Economic Times*, 'Tata's Supercomputer Eka Is the Fastest in Asia', 14 November 2007.

The Race

1. Lala, R.M. *Beyond the Last Blue Mountain*. Penguin India, 1993, pp. 85–89.
2. J.R.D. Tata's Journey Logbook, Tata Central Archives, Pune.
3. Letter from J.R.D. Tata to Air Vice Marshal A.M. Engineer, 19 October 1957, Tata Central Archives, Pune.

The Prime Minister's Relief Fund

1. Telegram sent by J.R.D. Tata to Jawaharlal Nehru, dated 14 August 1947, Tata Central Archives, Pune.
2. Letter from Jawaharlal Nehru to J.R.D. Tata, dated 11 December 1947, enclosing a note titled 'Note for a Proposed National Relief Fund', Tata Central Archives, Pune.

3. Tata Monthly Bulletin, Vol. 2, No. 11, 1947, p. 95, Tata Central Archives, Pune.
4. Lala, R.M. *Beyond the Last Blue Mountain*. Penguin India, 1993, pp. 325–26.

Tata, Birla and the Bombay Plan

1. *A Plan for Economic Development of India*. Bombay: Commercial Printing Press, 1944, pp. 1–55, Tata Central Archives, Pune.
2. 'A Fifteen-year Plan of Economic Development for India', a talk delivered to the Bombay Rotary Club on 15 February 1944 by Rotarian J.R.D. Tata, Tata Central Archives, Pune.
3. Notes on the Bombay Plan, Tata Economic Consultancy Services, Appendix 2.1, Tata Central Archives, Pune.
4. Lala, R.M. *Beyond the Last Blue Mountain*. Penguin India, 1993, pp. 219–24.

A Mission of Learning

1. Letter from J.R.D. Tata to Mahatma Gandhi, dated 9 May 1945, Tata Central Archives, Pune.
2. Letter from Mahatma Gandhi to J.R.D. Tata, dated 20 May 1945, Tata Central Archives, Pune.
3. Lala, R.M. *Beyond the Last Blue Mountain*. Penguin India, 1993, pp. 225–30.

Toilet Rolls and a Speech

1. Kohli, M.S. *JRD: As Air Indians Remember*. Himalayan Books, 2010, p. 93.
2. Lala, R.M. *Beyond the Last Blue Mountain*. Penguin India, 1993, pp. 344–45.

Lady Meherbai Tata: Feminist Icon

1   *Horizons: The Tata India Century, 1904–2004.* India Book House, 2004, pp. 127–28.
2. https://www.olympedia.org/athletes/1805026, Mehri Tata, biographical information.
3. Biodata of Meherbai Tata, Tata Central Archives, Pune.

Dr John Matthai: A Man of Many Parts

1. Lala, R.M. *Beyond the Last Blue Mountain.* Penguin India, 1993, pp. 207–08.
2. 'Family, Early Life and Education, Career', www.drjohnmatthai.com.
3. *Horizons: The Tata India Century, 1904–2004.* India Book House, 2004, p. 179.

A Temple for the Performing Arts

1. *Horizons: The Tata India Century, 1904-2004.* India Book House, 2004, pp. 218–20, 235.
2. NCPA, 27 May 2020, https://www.ncpamumbai.com/timeline.

Who Was Nevill Vintcent?

1. Lala, R.M. *Beyond the Last Blue Mountain.* Penguin India, 1993, pp. 91–92, 109.
2. Alikhan, Anvar. 'Air India's Forgotten Founding Father'. *Mint*, 11 July 2017.

People, First and Foremost

1. 'Industrial Relations: The TISCO Experience', text of speech delivered by Russi Mody at the auditorium of Bombay House, *Tata Review*, Vol. 16, No. 1, 1981.

2. *Sands of Time*, Tata Central Archives newsletter, Vol. 15, Issue 1, 2018, special commemorative issue on Russi Mody, pp. 1–6.
3. Sabharwal, Jyoti and Mukherjee, Partha. *Russi Mody: The Man Who Also Made Steel, a Biography.* Stellar Publishers, 2008.

The Maharajah Man

1. Lala, R.M. *Beyond the Last Blue Mountain.* Penguin India, 1993, pp. 119, 176–77.
2. 'Report on Farewell Function on Bobby Kooka's Retirement'. *Tata Review*, Vol. 8, No. 1, 1973, Tata Central Archives.
3. *Horizons: The Tata India Century, 1904-2004.* India Book House. 2004, pp. 238, 245.

Why Did Jamsetji Tata Build the Taj ?

1. Harris, Frank. *Jamsetji Nusserwanji Tata: A Chronicle of His Life.* Blackie & Sons, 1958, p. 72.
2. Dwivedi, Sharada and Allen, Charles. *The Taj at Apollo Bunder.* Pictor Publishing Pvt. Ltd, 2010, pp. 40–41.

Never Stop Dreaming

1. Harris, Frank. *Jamsetji Nusserwanji Tata: A Chronicle of His Life.* Blackie & Sons, 1958, pp. 91–112, 273–75.

An Eagle Takes to the Skies
1. Letter from J.R.D. Tata to Indira Gandhi, dated 1 July 1964, Tata Central Archives, Pune.
2. Speech delivered by J.R.D. Tata at the inauguration of the National Institute of Advanced Studies, 1988, Tata Central Archives, Pune.

3. National Institute of Advanced Studies Indian Institute of Science Campus, Bengaluru, 560 012, India. 'History', nias. res.in/content/history.

The Last Days of Jamsetji Tata

1. Harris, Frank. *Jamsetji Nusserwanji Tata: A Chronicle of His Life*. Blackie & Sons, 1958, pp. 266–76.
2. Lala, R.M. *For the Love of India: The Life and Times of Jamsetji Tata*. Penguin India, 2004, pp. 197–209.

A Legend with a Heart of Gold

1. *Sands of Time*, Tata Central Archives newsletter, Vol. 15, Issue 1, 2020, special commemorative issue on Darbari Seth, Vol. 17, Issue 1, 2020, pp. 9–11.

Tata Central Archives

For many of the stories you have read in this book, information and source material has been provided by the Tata Central Archives (TCA). Launched by J.R.D. Tata in 1991, TCA moved to its present location inaugurated by Ratan N. Tata in 2001 within the lush, green campus of the Tata Management Training Centre at Mangaldas Road, Pune.

TCA is a treasure trove of information on the Tata Group, ranging from the inception of the group in 1868 to the present time. It is a repository of important and rare documents, which are a rich source of information for any reader who has an interest in the history of the Tatas, their legendary leaders and India's industrialization.

Interesting offerings within TCA include an exact replication of J.R.D. Tata's Mumbai office, memorabilia such as chairs used by Jamsetji Tata, a memento gifted by Kalpana Chawla's family, and several visual displays that bring to life many aspects of the Tata Group's history and heritage.

TCA also offers, on its website, some virtual exhibitions which you can visit from the comfort of your home or office, including a beautifully curated exhibition on the life of Jamsetji Tata.

To know more, please do write to Tata Central Archives at tca@tata.com, or check out the website, http://www.tatacentralarchives.com/, or visit the archives in person.